THE INFANT TEACHER'S ASSEMBLY BOOK

THE
INFANT TEACHER'S
ASSEMBLY BOOK

edited by

D. M. PRESCOTT

LONDON

BLANDFORD PRESS

First published in 1954
2nd impression 1963
3rd impression 1970
4th impression 1974
© *Blandford Press*
167 *High Holborn, London, W.C.*1

ISBN 0 7137 0275 3

Printed in Great Britain by
Fletcher & Son Ltd, Norwich

CONTENTS

ACKNOWLEDGEMENTS

I am indebted to the following publishers and individuals from whom copyright material, as shown below, has been used:—

The Highway Press for the prayers "Dear God, we thank Thee for our families" (p. 17), "Dear Lord, we thank Thee for our mothers" (p. 17), "Our Father, thank You for all the people who love us" (p. 17), and "Our Father, we pray for Thy big family of children" (p. 17), from *All Our Friends*.

The Oxford University Press for the prayer "Lord, bless our school" (p. 18) and the hymn "Winter creeps" (p. 36) from *Prayers and Hymns for Junior Schools*.

Lilian McCrea for the verse "God is great" (p. 34).

Fleming H. Revell Company for the hymn "Winter day, frosty day" by Agnes R. Bacon (p. 36) from *The Hymnal for Boys and Girls*.

Hilda I. Rostron for the poem "Praise for baby creatures" (p. 38).

Basil Blackwell and the Rev. J. M. C. Crum for "In the morning early" (p. 39) and "To God who makes all lovely things" (p. 36) from *The Children's Kingdom*.

Simon & Schuster, Inc. and Artists and Writers Guild, Inc. for the poem "Thank You, God" (p. 35) by Leah Gale, from *Prayers for Children, A Little Golden Book*, copyright 1942.

John Morrison for "Christmas Song" (p. 40) from *Poems for People*.

Miss Stella Mead for "Playtime" (p. 43).

Allenson & Co. Ltd. for "The Pig Brother" (pp. 53–6) by Laura E. Richards from *The Golden Windows*.

The extracts from the Authorised Version of the Bible and the Book of Common Prayer, which are both Crown Copyright, are reproduced by permission.

The verse from *Acts* (p. 12) is from the Moffatt translation of the New Testament published by Hodder & Stoughton.

Considerable care has been taken in tracing the sources of copyright material, and it is regretted if any acknowledgements have been omitted.

D.M.P.

Miss E. Chapman, Headmistress, Lathom Primary Mixed School, East Ham, London, E. 7.

Mrs. Margaret Fox, N.F.F., Oatlands Park, Weybridge, Surrey.

Miss B. Goodall, Headmistress, The Dell Montessori School, Woking, Surrey.

Miss K. Hassell, Brim Hill, London, N.2.

Miss D. Heath, Headmistress, Boldmere County Infants' School, Sutton Coldfield, Warwickshire.

Miss Dorothy John, Wilton Crescent, London, S.W.1.

Miss Beryl Jones, Headmistress, Hafod-y-Wern County Infants' School, Queen's Park, Wrexham, Denbighshire.

Miss Kathleen Jukes, St. Christopher's School, Richmond Road, Horsham, Sussex.

Miss W. Nicholson, Headmistress, Brassey Street Infants' School, Birkenhead, Cheshire.

Miss B. Pedley, Forest Hill, London, S.E.23.

Miss M. E. Procter (writer of children's books), Manor Road, Barnet, Herts.

Miss B. M. Warman, Headmistress, Earl's Hall School, Westcliff-on-Sea, Essex.

Miss E. Weaver, Winton Infants' School, London, N.1.

Section 1

A PRIVATE PRAYER FOR TEACHERS
by Christina Rossetti

Lord Jesus, merciful and patient, grant us grace, we beseech Thee, ever to teach in a teachable spirit; learning along with those we teach, and learning from them whenever Thou so pleasest; that we and they may all be taught of God.

(*abridged*)

The Purpose of the Book

THE purpose of this volume is the same as that of the *Teacher's Assembly Book for Junior Schools* which preceded it—namely, to provide a source book from which leaders of Assemblies can compile for each day an act of worship which fits its special circumstances.

The *Junior Teacher's Assembly Book* was an experiment to see whether such a book could in fact be produced. Judging by reports which have come in from all over the country, the experiment appears to have succeeded; in fact, it is largely at the request of Infant teachers who have seen the Junior book and asked for something similar for their own schools that this new book has been compiled.

The same procedure was adopted as previously—that is, to work in consultation with those who were to use the book, and to ascertain what they themselves would most like to see in it. In so doing, it quickly became clear that something very different from the material provided in the Junior book was needed. It would not do merely to reduce the length and simplify the words of the prayers and readings. The whole process of infant education is based on *telling* as opposed to *reading*; and it was therefore necessary to produce the matter in a form which could be easily memorised and reproduced orally. For this reason, prayers have been chosen which are made-up of short sentences; and most of the prose stories are given in outline form, without much elaboration of detail, so that the teacher can fill in the background according to the need of the moment and the time available.

In talking to heads of schools, and those who habitually take Assemblies with Infants, it has been made clear that such Assemblies require above all things to be flexible. Often it is necessary to have an extended Assembly, when more is needed than a hymn and a prayer. To help to meet this need, dramatic hints have been included, as well as a number of extra stories to read or tell, and a full bibliography, largely built up from lists, sent in by teachers, of books which are favourites with their own children.

There will also be found a list of other books suitable for use in compiling Assemblies, including some which give a number of formal services, for those who find them useful.

D.M.P.

Section 2

Opening and Closing Sentences

*(Many schools will not need these; but some may,
and they are therefore included.)*

(A) OPENING SENTENCES

SECURITY IN GOD

(Jesus said), Lo, I am with you alway. (*Matthew* 28, 20.)

The Lord is my shepherd; I shall not want. (*Psalm* 23, 1.)

Whoso putteth his trust in the Lord shall be safe. (*Proverbs* 29, 25.)

(God said), Fear not; for I am with thee. (*Isaiah* 43, 5.)

Be strong and of a good courage. (*Joshua* 1, 18.)

(Jesus said), I am the good shepherd, and know my sheep. (*John* 10, 14.)

Our help is in the name of the Lord, who made heaven and earth. (*Psalm* 124, 8.)

LOVE FOR GOD

Thou shalt love the Lord thy God with all thy heart. (*Mark* 12, 30.)

We love (God), because he first loved us. (1 *John* 4, 19.)

WORSHIP

God is light; and in him is no darkness at all. (1 *John* 1, 5.)

The Lord is King for ever and ever. (*Psalm* 10, 16.)

HOW TO LIVE

Fight the good fight. (1 *Timothy* 6, 12.)

Be ye kind one to another . . . forgiving one another, even as God . . . hath forgiven you. (*Ephesians* 4, 32.)

(Jesus said), It is more blessed to give than to receive. (*Acts* 20, 35.)

To give is happier than to get. (*Acts* 20, 35, *Moffatt translation*.)

PRAYER

Speak, Lord; for thy servant heareth. (1 *Samuel* 3, 9.)

(Jesus said), Whatsoever ye shall ask in my name, that will I do. (*John* 14, 13.)

(B) CLOSING SENTENCES

The Lord shall preserve thy (our) going out and thy (our) coming in from this time forth, and even for evermore. (*Psalm* 121, 8.)

The blessing of God Almighty, the Father, the Son and the Holy Spirit, be upon us and remain with us forever. (*The Prayer Book*.)

From the rising of the sun unto the going down of the same the Lord's name . . . be praised. (*Psalm* 113, 3.)

The Lord be with you (us) all. Amen. (2 *Thessalonians* 3, 16.)

I will lay me down in peace, and take my rest; for it is Thou, Lord, only, that makest me dwell in safety. (*Psalm* 4, 9. P.B.V.)

When thou liest down, thou shalt not be afraid; yea, thou shalt lie down, and thy sleep shall be sweet. (*Proverbs* 3, 24.)

The Lord bless thee (us), and keep thee (us); the Lord make his face shine upon thee (us), and be gracious unto thee (us); the Lord lift up his countenance upon thee (us), and give thee (us) peace. (*Numbers* 6, 24–6.)

Section 3

Prayers

In gathering these prayers, it has been kept in mind how very short is the span of attention of small children. Wherever possible, prayers have been chosen or written which are built up from short sentences; in some cases, if the teacher so desires, they can be still further shortened by the omission of a sentence.

Many leaders of Assemblies may find it more satisfactory to make up their own prayers; they may like to have the written prayers as a basis from which to work.

It is being increasingly found, as will be seen from the teachers' experiences in Section 8, that even quite small people like to make up and pray their own simple petitions. These, of course, would be amplified and supplemented by the teacher's own prayers.

The prayers have been grouped as follows:—

For Special Times

Morning	A fine day
Evening	A wet day
Harvest	Play and games
Christmas	A grace before meals
Easter	

For Special People

Families	The big world family
Mothers	Sick children
Fathers	Animals and pets
Our school	

For Special Times

MORNING

May the blessing of God Almighty rest upon us and upon our work this day. *Amen.*

O Father God, we thank You for our sleep last night, and for our waking this morning ready for a new day. Please make it a happy day for us all. *Amen.*

O God, our Father, please be here in school with us to-day. Even if we cannot see You, help us to remember that You are near us always, taking care of us and helping us to do what is right. *Amen.*

Dear Father God, please bless us all to-day. Bless our work and our play; bless our singing and our story time; bless . . . (*whatever other activities are proposed*). Help us to do what is right today, so that we may make You happy; for Jesus' sake. *Amen.*

EVENING OR END OF SCHOOL DAY

Dear Father, school is over now, and we are going home. Help us to remember that Your love and care is all round us always, wherever we are. *Amen.*

Dear heavenly Father, we thank You for today, and all its work and fun. We thank You for all we have done—for . . . (*enumerate*). Please go with us when we go to our homes; for Jesus' sake. *Amen.*

Dear Lord, please watch over us and keep us safe this night. May Thine arms be round us, so that no harm can come to us. And bring us back to school to-morrow for another happy day. *Amen.*

HARVEST

Dear heavenly Father, we thank Thee that the harvest is safely gathered in. We thank Thee that there is corn in the barns for our bread, hay in the stacks to feed the cows which give us milk, and food in the shops for us to eat. Please bless all who have worked so hard for us so that we have all we need. *Amen.*

O Father God, we thank You for all the good gifts You give to Your children, for . . . (*enumerate*). Help us to be thankful to You always. *Amen.*

CHRISTMAS

Dear Father God, we thank You so much for sending Your Son, Baby Jesus, as Your Christmas present to the world. *Amen.*

Dear Father, we thank You for sending Jesus to us, to help us to be good and happy. Teach us to remember that He is with us always. *Amen.*

See also the special Christmas prayers on p. 20

EASTER

Dear Father God, we thank Thee for the happy time of Easter, when everything is new—new leaves on the trees, new nests for the birds, new lambs in the fields. We thank Thee that because Jesus died for us and came back to life again on Easter Day, we can have new hearts too. *Amen.*

Dear loving Father, we are thinking this morning of Jesus Christ, who died on a cross. We are very sorry that this happened to Him, and we want very much not to hurt Him any more. Help us to love Him and stand up for Him, and to do what He wants us to do, all our lives. We ask it for His sake. *Amen.*

Dear loving Father, we come to thank Thee this morning for raising Jesus Christ from the dead. We come with joy, for we know that nothing bad could kill Him for always.

We thank Thee that He came back to forgive Peter for saying that he did not know Him, and to forgive all His friends for running away. Help us always to come to Thee to be forgiven for all we do wrong. *Amen.*

(After hearing the story of Saint Peter's denial)

Dear Father, we have heard the story of Peter, who thought he was brave, and then was not brave at all. Please will You help us when we are frightened? Be with us when we are alone. Help us to tell the truth, even when it is very hard, so that we may not have to be sorry afterwards, as Peter was. We ask it in Jesus' name. *Amen.*

FOR A FINE DAY

Dear Father, we thank Thee for this lovely sunny day. Help us to be happy in it for Thee. *Amen.*

FOR A WET DAY

Dear Father God, we thank Thee for sending the rain to give the thirsty flowers a drink and make the green things grow. Help us to be happy indoors, and to work and play so that we make Thee happy too. *Amen.*

PLAY AND GAMES

O Lord our Father, please be with us in all our games and play. Help us to play fair, and take turns, and have a happy time with nothing to spoil it. *Amen.*

A GRACE BEFORE MEALS

For health and strength and daily food we praise Thy name, O Lord.

For Special People

FOR HOMES AND FAMILIES

Dear God, we thank Thee for our families; for fathers and mothers, brothers and sisters. Help us to be kind and loving in our homes, so that we make other people glad. *Amen.*

FOR MOTHERS

Dear Lord, we thank Thee for our mothers. We thank Thee for all the loving things they do for us. Help us to help them all we can. *Amen.*

Our Father, thank You for all the people who love us, especially our mothers. Help us to be loving too, and to show our love for them by the kind and helpful things we do. *Amen.*

FOR FATHERS

Dear heavenly Father, we thank Thee for our own fathers. Be with them today, in all the work they have to do. Keep them safe and make them happy; for Jesus' sake. *Amen.*
(For other prayers for parents, see the special prayers for Christmas, p. 20.)

FOR THE BIG WORLD FAMILY OF CHILDREN

Our Father, we pray for Thy big family of children in all the world. Help us to remember that Thou are our Father, and that all boys and girls everywhere belong to Thy family. *Amen.*

SPECIAL PETITIONS

FOR OUR SCHOOL

Lord, bless our school; so that working together and playing together, we may learn to serve Thee and to serve one another; for Jesus' sake. *Amen.*

FOR SICK CHILDREN

Dear Father, bless . . . who is ill. Be close to him (her), and make him (her) better soon. *Amen.*

FOR ANIMALS AND PETS

Dear heavenly Father, we thank Thee for all the animals, . . . (*enumerate*). Teach us to be kind to them, and to care for them, so that they will know that we are their friends. *Amen.*

(After a "saint" animal story—see p 61)

Dear Father, help us to care for animals and birds as Saint . . . did. May we be kind and loving to all the creatures that we meet, and specially to our pets; for Jesus' sake. *Amen.*

Special Petitions

FOR LIKENESS TO JESUS 3·11·78·

Dear God, thank You for sending Jesus into the world. Help us to remember that He is still here, even if we cannot see Him, and that if we listen we can hear Him speaking to us in our hearts. Help us to listen, and then do what He tells us. *Amen.*

O God our Father, we are thinking today of Jesus when He was a little boy. We remember how He lived in His home in Nazareth with Joseph and Mary. We remember how He loved them and obeyed them and did all He could to help them. Show us how to be like Jesus in our homes and at school. *Amen.*

FOR KNOWLEDGE OF RIGHT AND WRONG

Loving Father, please tell us when we are doing wrong things, and help us to say we are sorry. *Amen.*

FOR FORGIVENESS

Dear Father, Thou knowest that we are not always good; we sometimes do and say things that make Thee sad. Please forgive us; help us to say we are sorry for those wrong things, and not do them any more, so that we may make Thee happy again. *Amen.*

FOR POWER TO HEAR GOD'S VOICE

Our Father God, teach us to listen for Thy voice, which tells us to do kind and loving things for our friends; and when we hear, help us to obey. *Amen.*

FOR POWER TO BE GRATEFUL

Dear Father God, You have given us so many things to make us happy. (*Here the teacher can mention some which the children will specially appreciate.*) Help us to share our good things with others, so that they may be happy too. *Amen.*

Our Father God, we thank Thee for all Thy loving, protecting care. Thou hast been very good to us. Make us kind and thoughtful, and careful of all that Thou hast given to us. *Amen.*

FOR HELP IN USING OUR BODIES RIGHTLY

Dear Father, thank You for giving us our bodies to take care of and use for You. Thank You for our busy feet and our useful hands, our eyes, which can see such lovely things, and our ears, which can hear songs and stories and other happy sounds. Help us to take good care of all that You have given us. *Amen.*

Five Prayers for the Five School Days Before Christmas

(*as used in a school in the north-west*)

FIRST DAY

Dear loving Father, we thank Thee for Christmas time, when we think about Baby Jesus, who was born in the stable, because there was no room anywhere else. We think of Mary, His gentle mother, and Joseph who cared for them both. Help us at this time to remember Jesus, and to grow more like Him day by day. *Amen.*

SECOND DAY

Dear Father in heaven, we think this morning of Mary, the mother of Jesus, who wrapped Him up and laid Him in a manger. We think of all the mothers in the world who care for little children. Help us to love and care for our mothers, as Jesus did when He grew up in His home in Nazareth. *Amen.*

THIRD DAY

Dear Father, today we think of Joseph, the kind man who took care of Mary on her long journey to Bethlehem. We think of our own fathers, and how they take care of us. Help us to grow up strong and good, like Joseph; for Jesus' sake. *Amen.*

FOURTH DAY

Dear Father God, we think today of the shepherds in the fields, to whom the angels brought the news about the Baby Jesus. We remember how they went to find Him in the stable, and how glad they were when they found Him lying in a manger. Help us to be glad too, and to make other people happy this Christmas. *Amen.*

FIFTH DAY

Dear Father God, we are thinking today of the three wise kings who came a long way to find Baby Jesus, bowing before

Him and giving Him rich presents. Help us to think of kind things to do this Christmas, and of presents we can give to our friends; for Jesus' sake. *Amen.*

Notes on Explaining the Lord's Prayer to Small Children

(as used in a Surrey school. The ideas can be adapted to suit the circumstances of any school or class)

OUR FATHER WHICH ART IN HEAVEN

God is our Father in heaven—our heavenly Father. He loves everyone everywhere, and each one of you, too, just like your fathers love you. Only God's love is much bigger than Father's love or Mother's love. Mothers and fathers sometimes have to go away; but God is there always. Even though we can't see Him, we know He is there, caring for us and keeping us safe.

HALLOWED BE THY NAME

"Hallowed" means "holy" or "special". God's name is very special. Our mothers and fathers are very special to us, and the Queen is very special indeed, but God is the most special of all, and we must love Him, just as we do our mothers and fathers, and the Queen, and all the other people we love.

THY KINGDOM COME, THY WILL BE DONE, ON EARTH AS IT IS IN HEAVEN

We are asking God to help all the world—that means, all the people everywhere. God wants all the people in the world to live His way, which is the happy way. If we listen to Him, and ask Him to help us, He will show us how to live God's way.

When you or I quarrel with our brothers and sisters, or are rude to our mothers, or do any of the things that we know we ought not to do, then we are spoiling God's way, and helping to make the world unhappy.

THE LORD'S PRAYER

GIVE US THIS DAY OUR DAILY BREAD

This means that we are asking God to give us all the food we need for today, not only bread, but all the other things we need as well.

AND FORGIVE US OUR TRESPASSES, AS WE FORGIVE THEM THAT TRESPASS AGAINST US

"Trespass" is a difficult big word; but it just means all the things we do that we know we ought not to do, like being cross or not doing what Mother or the teacher tells us, or fighting, or hurting someone. We say we are sorry to God— as you do to your mother sometimes—for the bad things we have done. We ask Him to forgive us and make us happy again; but then we, too, must be ready to forgive other people, and love them, when they have done unkind things to us.

LEAD US NOT INTO TEMPTATION, BUT DELIVER US FROM EVIL

When we say these words, we are asking God to help us to do what He wants, and to make us strong, so that we can fight the bad things and do what is right.

FOR THINE IS THE KINGDOM, THE POWER AND THE GLORY, FOR EVER AND EVER. AMEN

When we say these words, we are saying that we know God is the ruler or King over everything—that He is the most wonderful "Person" there is—and that He lives for ever and ever.

This is hard for us to understand, because our minds and brains—the thinking part inside us that we can't see—are so small. They are quite good enough for this world, but they aren't good enough to understand all about God and Heaven. One day God will give us minds that can understand all these things; but now all we have to do is to love God and trust Him, and know that He will look after us always.

Section 4

Prayers and Praises
with Responses

These little praises, prayers and responses have been put together with the intention that they should be used either whole or in part. Some phrases will be found to be more useful at one time of the year than another; some for one age more than for another; others, in one particular part of the country more than in another. They do not aim to cover the whole gamut of a child's life, but may suggest a line that can be followed by the teacher.

In all cases children can add their own petitions and thank You's, which will make the prayer time personal to them. A quiet pause, introduced by some such phrase as "God is here; let us hear what He has to say, and speak to Him in our hearts", can lead on to such a time.

There may be a new baby in the family, a birthday in the class, some new members of the school, new swings in the park, or new flowers in the fields, for which they would like to thank God, so bringing Him into every phase of their daily lives. They may have something for which they want to say they are sorry to Him, or someone they want to ask Him to bless.

The responses can be varied, using such other phrases as:

> We thank Thee, O Father.
> Thank You, Heavenly Father.
> We give Thee our thanks.
> Bless us and help us.
> Hear our prayers, O God.

Worship

Praise

Thank You, our Father God, because You loved us so much that You gave us our Lord Jesus, Your Son, to be our Friend, and to give His life for us.

RESPONSE.—*Thank You, thank You, God.*

Thank You that he was born a Baby, as we were; that He cried and laughed as we do, and grew and became strong, and played with His friends, and obeyed His mother Mary, and worked with Joseph in the carpenter's shop, and went to school to learn lessons.

RESPONSE.—*Thank You, thank You, God.*

Thank You that after He grew up, He went about doing good to everyone, showing them what You are like, and teaching them how they should live with one another and love one another.

RESPONSE.—*Thank You, thank You, God.*

Thank You that He gave His life for all of us, and rose again on Easter Day, and lives now to help us all to live as He lived.

RESPONSE.—*Thank You, thank You, God.*

Prayer

O God our Father, help us to live as Jesus showed us how to live. Help us to be honest in all we say and do, thoughtful and obedient; to be pure in thought and word and deed; to love each other as Jesus loved us; and to think of ourselves last.

RESPONSE.—*Help us, good Lord.*

School

Praise

Thank You, our Father God, for our school, where we learn about the world You made, and how to live in it.

RESPONSE.—*Thank You, thank You, God.*

Thank You for the lessons we learn, the stories we hear, the games we play, and the songs we sing. Thank You . . .

> for hard work done,
> for difficult things won,
> and for all our fun.

RESPONSE.—*Thank You, thank You, God.*

Thank You for the joy that comes when we have done a good piece of work, even if it means doing it over and over again until it is right, as Jesus did in the carpenter's shop.

RESPONSE.—*Thank You, thank You, God.*

Thank You for the happy times we have when we do things together, and share everything with each other. Thank You for all our friends.

RESPONSE.—*Thank You, thank You, God.*

10·5·96

Prayer

Teach us, good Lord, to serve You in school with all our hearts. Help us to obey our teachers, to enjoy hard work, and to play fair. Help us not to mind whether we win or lose, but to do our best: help us not to make a fuss when we are hurt. Make us friendly, brave, honest and unselfish.

> Give us eyes to see,
> ears to hear,
> fingers to work.

RESPONSE.—*Help us, good Lord.*

Our Families

Praise

Thank You, our Father God, for families and homes; thank You for fathers who work hard for us, so that we can have food to eat, and clothes to wear, and houses to live in; thank You for mothers who love us and have looked after us

25

ever since we were babies; who listen to us when we talk, and comfort us when we are sad, and play and laugh with us when we are glad; who sew and bake and wash and make for us, and care for us all the day long.

RESPONSE.—*Thank You, thank You, God.*

Thank You for older brothers and sisters, and younger brothers and sisters, for new babies who belong to all of us, and for all the good gifts You have given to us in our family life at home.

RESPONSE.—*Thank You, thank You, God.*

Thank You for grandfathers and grandmothers, for uncles and aunts, and for all our relations.

RESPONSE.—*Thank You, thank You, God.*

Prayer

O God, the Father of all families, make our family like the family where Jesus grew up, and our home like His home, where we all care for each other, and share our things with each other, so that there is enough for everyone. Show us what to do when we feel jealous, or want our own way, or don't want to help.

RESPONSE.—*Help us, good Lord.*

Ourselves

Praise

Thank You, our Father God, for so wonderfully making us; for giving us bodies, and hands, and arms, legs, and feet, and for making us strong to run about and use our limbs.

RESPONSE.—*Thank You, thank You, God.*

Thank You for giving us eyes to see and ears to hear, lips and tongues to speak and laugh and sing; teeth to eat with, and a good appetite for the food You give us day by day.

RESPONSE.—*Thank You, thank You, God.*

Thank You for the water we wash and bathe in, the clothes we dress in, the beds we sleep in, and the houses we live in.

RESPONSE.—*Thank You, thank You, God.*

Prayer

Help us, good Lord, to keep our bodies and souls clean and pure for You. Forgive us all our sins, and help us to be different, not to be always thinking of what we like and don't like, whom we like and don't like. Keep us from being angry, or sulky, or obstinate, or unkind. Make us good neighbours to every one. Give us happy and loving hearts, that we may turn all our enemies into friends, and all our friends into better friends.

RESPONSE.—*Help us, good Lord.*

Nature

Praise

Thank You, our Father God, for clouds and sunshine, the rain that washes the earth and makes things grow, the wind that makes roots go down strongly into the earth.

RESPONSE.—*Thank You, thank You, God.*

Thank You for the *spring*, and for everything waking; for black buds on the trees, and the green sap rising, for swinging catkin, and breaking leaf, for opening flowers, and for blossom on the fruit trees. Thank You for birds singing all day long, and for the baby creatures in the farms and fields and woods and streams.

(*The children may like to add here any new flower seen, the first cuckoo, etc.*)

RESPONSE.—*Thank You, thank You, God.*

Thank You for the *summer*, for the fruit ripening in the orchards and gardens, and the hay and corn ripening in the fields. Thank You for garden flowers and wild flowers. Thank You for warmth and sunshine, and for summer holidays. Thank

You for the country; for green fields and hedges, for streams and rivers where we can fish, for hills and mountains. Thank You for parks and playgrounds, for swings and see-saws and merry-go-rounds. Thank You for the seaside; for the sea where we bathe and paddle, and the sands where we build castles and pies; for little pools among the rocks, for star-fish and shells and sea-anemones.

RESPONSE.—*Thank You, thank You, God.*

Thank You for the *autumn*; for the harvest gathered in to feed us in the winter, and to give us our daily bread. Thank You for golden corn, and red apples, for purple plums, and brown nuts. Thank You for the leaves changing colour on the trees, then falling down to feed the earth and to make room for the new leaves coming; thank You for the crackle of the flames and the blue smoke of bonfires in our gardens.

RESPONSE.—*Thank You, thank You, God.*

Thank you for the *winter*, for ice and snow and frost, for games to play in the snow, and patterns on the window-pane, and for all the seeds and roots safely asleep in the earth.

RESPONSE.—*Thank You, thank You, God.*

Thank You for all the beautiful sounds and smells and colours around us. Thank You for the different songs and calls of the birds, for the sounds of the wind in the trees, and the waves on the beach, and the pattering rain. Thank You for the different scents of the flowers, of green larches and pines in the sun, of new-mown grass, of earth after rain, and of wood smoke. Thank You for all the different colours of flowers, for the green of trees and grass, the gold of ripe corn, and the blue of the sky.

RESPONSE.—*Thank You, thank You, God.*

Prayer

Teach us, good Lord, to love the world that You have made, and never to grumble at the weather. May we help You to look after the beautiful things You have given us for our pleasure, and never spoil or hurt them. Bless all who tend the earth, to give us food, so that there may be a good harvest.

RESPONSE.—*Help us, good Lord.*

Night and Day

Praise

Thank You, O God who made Day and Light and saw that they were good, for all the sunshine and light of the day, when we can run around and play, eat our food, and learn our lessons, and see all the good things that You have made for us to enjoy.

RESPONSE.—*Thank You, thank You, God.*

Thank You, O God who made Night and Darkness and saw that they were good, for the quiet, safe dark which folds us round like a cloak, making it easy for us to sleep; for the stars that shine and twinkle, and for the moon's soft light. Thank You for sleep, when we grow strong for the morning.

RESPONSE.—*Thank You, thank You, God.*

Prayer

Be near us, good Lord, both in our sleeping and in our waking, that sleeping we may rest in safety, and waking we may praise You with joyful hearts.

RESPONSE.—*Help us, good Lord.*

For All Who Look After Us

Praise

Thank You, O God our Helper, for all who help You to look after us.

RESPONSE.—*Thank You, thank You, God.*

For mothers and fathers, and all who look after us in our homes.

RESPONSE.—*Thank You, thank You, God.*

For teachers who help us at school, and for all who teach us what You are like, in Church and Chapel and in Sunday School.

RESPONSE.—*Thank You, thank You, God.*

For doctors and nurses who look after us when we are ill, and for chemists who mix medicines to make us well again. For health visitors and dentists, for first-aid workers and ambulance drivers, and for dustbin men.

RESPONSE.—*Thank You, thank You, God.*

For policemen and firemen and all who guard us and our homes and keep us safe; for soldiers and sailors and airmen who defend us; for lighthouse keepers and coastguards who guard our ships and shores.

RESPONSE.—*Thank You, thank You, God.*

For miners who dig coal to keep us warm; for the men who build our houses and make our furniture.

RESPONSE.—*Thank You, thank You, God.*

For train drivers and bus drivers, who take us safely when we are travelling.

RESPONSE.—*Thank You, thank You, God.*

For farmers and fishermen, for shepherds and herdsmen, for fruit growers and gardeners, for bakers who get up very early to bake our bread, and for all who catch or make our food. For the men who bring it safely over the seas, the lorry-drivers who often carry it such a long way and the shopkeepers who sell it to us.

RESPONSE.—*Thank You, thank You, God.*

(Pause here for children to add other thank You's for all
who look after us)

Prayer

O God our Father, who all our lives dost help us and defend us, give us thankful hearts for all who look after us, and help us to work with them to make the world a safe and happy place, where everyone can live without fear.

RESPONSE.—*Help us, good Lord.*

For All Helpful Things

Praise

Thank You, God, for all the things that clever people make to help us.

    RESPONSE.—*Thank You, thank You, God.*

Thank You for trains and trams, for buses and trolley buses, for cars and bicycles, for planes and ships, which carry us quickly and safely from one place to another.

    RESPONSE.—*Thank You, thank You, God.*

Thank You for fires to warm us, and for all the different ways our food is cooked, or kept cold and good. Thank You for hot water to wash in and bath in. Thank You for lights in our homes and in the streets.

    RESPONSE.—*Thank You, thank You, God.*

Thank You for wireless and telephones and television, for the cinema, and for all the wonderful things made for our pleasure.

    RESPONSE.—*Thank You, thank You, God.*

Prayer

Teach us, good Lord, to take care of all the good things You have given us to help us.

    RESPONSE.—*Help us, good Lord.*

The World Family

Praise

Thank You, our Father God, that You have made the world with so many different kinds of people in it, with different languages, and colours, and ways of living, like a garden full of different flowers.

    RESPONSE.—*Thank You, thank You, God.*

Thank You that, though we look so different, we are all like each other inside, that we all have bodies that need food and clothes, minds that think, and hearts that feel; thank You that everywhere, all over the world, there are families that love each other, mothers and fathers, boys and girls, and babies.

RESPONSE.—*Thank You, thank You, God.*

(A pause, to pray for any we know, of another race.)

Thank You, good Lord, that every person and every nation has something to give to the world, to make it the place you meant it to be, whether we are white or black or brown or yellow.

RESPONSE.—*Thank You, thank You, God.*

(Pause again for any special thank You for what any nation has given to the world. This might link up with what the children have been learning in geography.)

Prayer

Teach us, good Lord, to see the world as one big family of brothers and sisters, with one Father, God. Help us to work together and to care for one another, that all may give their best, and look after any who may be in need.

RESPONSE.—*Help us, good Lord.*

(Silent pause again here, for the children to think of any lonely person of another race or their own race, in their class at school or in their street, whom they could help.)

A Thank You Song

Say thank you to God, for He is good:

RESPONSE.—*For He is kind for ever and ever.*

Say thank you to the God of everything:

RESPONSE.—*For He is kind for ever and ever.*

Say thank you to the God of everybody:

RESPONSE.—*For He is kind for ever and ever.*

To God who made the sky:

RESPONSE.—*For He is kind for ever and ever.*

To God who made the earth and sea:

RESPONSE.—*For He is kind for ever and ever.*

To God who made the sun and moon and stars:
    RESPONSE.—*For He is kind for ever and ever.*
The sun to rule by day:
    RESPONSE.—*For He is kind for ever and ever.*
The moon and the stars to rule by night:
    RESPONSE.—*For He is kind for ever and ever.*
To God who chose our country to serve Him: •
    RESPONSE.—*For He is kind for ever and ever.*
And gave us all the beautiful things in it:
    RESPONSE.—*For He is kind for ever and ever.*
Who has kept us safe all these years:
    RESPONSE.—*For He is kind for ever and ever.*
And has given us wise and good men to rule over us:
    RESPONSE.—*For He is kind for ever and ever.*
Who taught us how to care for each other:
    RESPONSE.—*For He is kind for ever and ever.*
And gave us churches, hospitals and schools:
    RESPONSE.—*For He is kind for ever and ever.*
Who has made green fields and orchards:
    RESPONSE.—*For He is kind for ever and ever.*
Rivers, and trees, and mountains for our joy:
    RESPONSE.—*For He is kind for ever and ever.*
Who remembered us when we most needed Him:
    RESPONSE.—*For He is kind for ever and ever.*
And saved us from all that made us afraid:
    RESPONSE.—*For He is kind for ever and ever.*
Who gives food to everyone:
    RESPONSE.—*For He is kind for ever and ever.*
Say thank you to the God of heaven:
    RESPONSE.—*For He is kind for ever and ever.*

                                (Based on Psalm 136.)

Section 5

Verse

(A) SHORT VERSES

General

AS HAPPY AS KINGS
The world is so full
  Of a number of things,
I'm sure we should all
  Be as happy as kings.
                    R. L. Stevenson

God is great,
  And we are small;
Yet He loves
  And needs us all.

GOOD, BETTER, BEST
Good, better, best—
May we never rest
Till the good is better,
And the better's best.
                    Old Rhyme

A LITTLE THANK YOU
Thank you, Jesus Lord, for all—
  Stars that twinkle, birds that sing,
Running hoop, and bouncing ball,
  Drums that rumble, bells that ring.
                    M. E. Procter

34

A LITTLE PRAYER

Hear me as I come to Thee;
Father God, be near to me.
All Thy little children bless.
Please forgive my naughtiness.
Make and keep me pure within,
Clean and free from every sin. *Amen.*

M. E. Procter

Nature

THANK YOU, GOD

God made the sun,
    And God made the tree,
God made the mountains,
    And God made me.

I thank You, O God,
    For the sun and the tree,
For making the mountains
    And for making me.

Leah Gale

WHO HAS SEEN THE WIND?

Who has seen the wind?
    Neither you nor I;
But when the trees bow down their heads,
    The wind is passing by.

Who has seen the wind?
    Neither I nor you;
But when the leaves hang trembling,
    The wind is passing through.

Christina Rossetti

SHORT VERSES

WINTER

Winter creeps,
Nature sleeps;
Birds are gone,
Flowers are none.
Fields are bare,
Bleak the air,
Leaves are shed;
All seems dead.

God's alive!
Grow and thrive.
Hidden away
Bloom of May,
Rose of June;
Very soon
Nought but green
Will be seen.

Percy Dearmer

SNOW

On winter nights the quiet flakes
Come falling, falling all the night
And when the world next morning wakes
It finds itself in robes of white.

The Rev. J. M. C. Crum

WINTER DAY

Winter day, frosty day!
God a cloak on all doth lay.
On the earth the snow He sheddeth,
On the lamb a fleece He spreadeth,
Gives the bird a coat of feather
To protect it from the weather,
Gives the children home and food.
Let us praise Him; God is good!

Agnes R. Bacon

GRATITUDE

To God who makes all lovely things,
How happy must our praises be.
Each day a new surprise He brings,
To make us glad His world to see.

The Rev. J. M. C. Crum

ON A RAINY DAY

God sends the rain
  To help to grow the wheat;
The wheat is made into the bread
  For all of us to eat.
Let's thank our Father God
  For sending us the rain,
And when the fields have had enough,
  For stopping it again.

D.M.P.

HARVEST TIME

Harvest time is here again.
Farmers cut the golden grain;
Busy fingers gather hops,
Or the plum and apple crops.
God has given us winter food.
Let us thank Him; He is good.

D.M.P.

A SONG OF SPRING

God has sent the spring again.
Gone are winter cold and rain.
Gay spring flowers show their faces;
Birds are choosing nesting places.
Everything is fresh and new—
Let us all be happy too.

D.M.P.

37

Birds and Beasts

PRAISE FOR BABY CREATURES

For chicks that cheep at clucking hens
   and rooster's "Cock-a-doo",
For piglets pink that run and squeal
   and leggy calves that moo:

For barking puppies, baa-ing lambs,
   and mewing kittens' ways;
For quacking ducklings on the pond:
   we give to Thee our praise.
Hilda I. Rostron

LITTLE THINGS

Thank you for all happy things:
   Frisking lambs, and dancing foals,
   Baby fish in shining shoals,
Butterflies with painted wings.

Thank you, Lord, for baby snails,
   Baby crabs, and tiny frogs,
   Kittens, calves, and puppy dogs,
Baby pigs with curly tails.

Lord, I pray that I may be
   Careful for their littleness,
   So that I, with them, may bless
You who made us young and free.
M. E. Procter

Dear Father, hear, and bless
   The beasts and singing birds,
And guard with tenderness
   Small things that have no words.

BIRD SONGS

In the early morning,
  Listen to the lark,
Singing in the daylight,
  Singing out the dark.
In the early springtime
  Hear the thrushes sing,
Singing out the winter,
  Singing in the spring.
Jesus loves the lilies,
  Jesus loves the birds;
They'd be singing with us
  If they knew the words.
O let us say clearly
  What they try to say—
Birds and buds and babies
  Thanking Him today.
                    The Rev. J. M. C. Crum

LITTLE LAMB

Little lamb, who made thee?
Dost thou know who made thee?
Gave thee life and bade thee feed
By the stream and o'er the mead,
Gave thee clothing of delight,
Softest clothing, woolly, bright;
Gave thee such a tender voice,
Making all the vales rejoice;
Little lamb, who made thee?
Dost thou know who made thee?

Little lamb, I'll tell thee;
Little lamb, I'll tell thee.
He is callèd by thy name,
For He calls Himself a lamb.
He is meek and He is mild.
He became a little child,
I a child, and thou a lamb,
We are callèd by His name.
Little lamb, God bless thee!
Little lamb, God bless thee!
                    William Blake

39

Christmas Verse

CHRISTMAS SONG

Softly, softly
Come to the manger and see Him.
Holy, holy
Peace He has come to restore.
Gently, gently
Mary His mother will hold Him.
Humbly, humbly
Shepherds and wise men adore.

John Morrison

THE GREEN GRASS CAROL

There grew in a field some grass so green,
    On Christmas Day, on Christmas Day,
The greenest grass that ever was seen,
    On Christmas Day in the morning.

That grass so green was fit for a king,
    On Christmas Day, on Christmas Day,
And then there happened a wonderful thing,
    On Christmas Day in the morning.

That grass was cut and made into hay,
    On Christmas Day, on Christmas Day,
And on it the Baby Jesus lay,
    On Christmas Day in the morning.

John Oliver

A LITTLE CAROL

If I were a little lamb,
On the night the angels came,
I would run to Bethlehem
    And see the Baby Jesus.

If I were a little star,
Shining on that stable bare,
I would send my brightness there
    To light the Baby Jesus.

If I were a little ass,
Tethered in that stable place,
I would see His sleeping face,
    And watch the Baby Jesus.

Though I am not ass nor lamb,
Nor a star of Bethlehem,
I a child, just as I am,
    Can love the Baby Jesus.

                      D.M.P.

(B) LONGER POEMS

THE FRIENDLY BEASTS

(*This poem might be used as a corporate act of worship at Christmas time, the verses being learnt by separate classes and then put together. If the last verse is too difficult, the first verse might be repeated at the end*)

Jesus our brother, strong and good,
Was humbly born in a stable rude,
And the friendly beasts around Him stood—
Jesus our brother, strong and good.

"I," said the donkey, shaggy and brown,
"I carried His mother up hill and down,
"I carried her safely to Bethlehem town;
"I," said the donkey, shaggy and brown.

"I," said the cow, all white and red,
"I gave Him my manger for His bed,
"I gave Him my hay to pillow His head;
"I," said the cow, all white and red.

"I," said the sheep with curly horn,
"I gave Him my wool for His blanket warm;
"He wore my coat on Christmas morn;
"I," said the sheep with curly horn.

"I," said the dove from the rafters high,
"I cooed Him to sleep that He should not cry.
"We cooed Him to sleep, my mate and I;
"I," said the dove from the rafters high.

And every beast, by some good spell,
In the stable dark was glad to tell
Of the gift he gave Immanuel,
The gift he gave Immanuel.

Robert Davis

PLAYTIME

When Christ was born in Bethlehem
The bells of heaven rang,
And high above His stable bed
The holy angels sang.

But He became a simple Child
Who laughed and played like me,
And knelt at night to say His prayers
Beside His mother's knee.

If I had lived in Nazareth
When he was very small
We might have played as little friends,
With whip and top, or ball.

I wonder if in Joseph's shop
He liked to push the plane?
And if He lost His father's tools
And found them once again?

And did He pick the shavings up
That lay upon the ground,
And wonder at the curly things,
And twist them round and round?

He reigns as Lord of Heaven now,
And Christmas bells shall ring,
And every child shall sing a song,
To Jesus Christ the King.

But when I kneel on Christmas Eve
And fold my hands to pray,
I'll think of Jesus once on earth
A little child at play.

Stella Mead

MISTER NOBODY

I know a funny little man,
        As quiet as a mouse,
Who does the mischief that is done
        In everybody's house!
There's no one ever sees his face,
        And yet we all agree
That every plate we break was cracked
        By Mister Nobody.

'Tis he who always tears our books,
        Who leaves the doors ajar,
He pulls the buttons from our clothes,
        And scatters pins afar;
That squeaky door will always squeak,
        Because of this, you see—
We leave the oiling to be done
        By Mister Nobody.

The finger-marks upon the door
        By none of *us* are made;
We never leave the blinds undrawn
        To let the curtains fade;
The ink *we* never spill; the boots
        That lying round you see
Are not *our* boots; they all belong
        To Mister Nobody.

                                        Anonymous

Section 6

Readings

(1.) BIBLE STORIES—STORIES OF JESUS

THE STORY OF ZACCHAEUS (*Za-keè-us*)   *Luke* 19, 1–10

There was once a little man called Zacchaeus, who was very greedy. He always wanted fine clothes, and lovely food, and lots and lots of money. To get these things he used to rob and cheat people; and he went on doing that till he was very rich.

But though he was so rich, he was not happy. He was so cross that nobody wanted him as a friend; and all the people whose money he took hated him. People laughed at him too, because he was so little; and all his money could not make him any bigger. So he was very lonely and unhappy.

Then one day Zacchaeus heard that Jesus was coming to his town. He wanted to see Jesus very much. He had heard stories about Him, and these stories said that Jesus could make ill people well. It was said too that Jesus could make unhappy people happy. So Zacchaeus went off to wait by the roadside for Jesus.

But when he got there, there were so many people all crowding together that poor little Zacchaeus couldn't see through them. He tried to push his way through; but nobody liked him, and so nobody would make a place for him. At last he climbed up into a sycamore tree to be able to see Jesus. And when the people saw him up there, how they laughed!

"Look at little Zacchaeus," they cried, "up in that tree! Doesn't he look silly?"

Just then Jesus came by, and looked up and saw Zacchaeus. But He did not laugh. He said, "Zacchaeus, make haste and come down; for I should like to have dinner at your house today." So down came little Zacchaeus as quickly as he could. How proud and happy he was that Jesus wanted to be his friend and come to his house for dinner!

But the other people were not pleased. "Why has Jesus gone to dinner with a bad man?" they grumbled. "Why did He not go to the good people?" Zacchaeus heard what they were saying; so he stopped, and said to Jesus, "I will give the half of all I have, Lord, to the poor people; and if I have cheated anyone, I will give him back four times as much." Zacchaeus was so happy to have Jesus as his friend, that he was going to be good, and not bad any more.

Then they went to his home, and had a wonderful dinner. And Zacchaeus knew that God had forgiven him for all his badness, and that Jesus would be his friend for always and always.

THE BOY WHO GAVE JESUS HIS DINNER   *John* 6, 1–13

There was once a boy who wanted to hear Jesus talking. So he went out to find Him. Before he started, his mother packed him up a picnic lunch, five little loaves and two small fishes. He carried it in a little basket. Then he set out.

He found Jesus sitting on a grassy hill, with a big crowd of people round Him, listening to Him talking. He was telling them wonderful stories about God, their heavenly Father. They liked listening to Him so much that they sat there all day long, till it was past supper time.

Jesus had some friends with Him, called disciples; and Jesus said to them, "I am sorry for all these people—they have been with Me a long time, and they have nothing to eat. We must not send them away hungry."

"But," said His friends the disciples, "how can we get enough bread out here in the country for all these people?"

"How many loaves have you got?" said Jesus.

So they went to look; and all they could find was the boy's little picnic—the five loaves, no bigger than rolls, and the two small fish. They brought them to Jesus, saying, "They won't be much use among so many." But Jesus told all the people to sit down on the grass. Then He took the loaves and fish, and said a prayer of thanks to God for them; then He broke them up and put the pieces in one of the baskets the people had brought their food in, before they had eaten it all up. The disciples carried the baskets round, and gave food to the hungry men and women, boys and girls. And in some wonderful way there was enough for everyone, for Jesus and His disciples too, and for the boy who had brought the picnic. There was even some left over, which they picked up in baskets so as not to waste it.

Then after that good supper, Jesus sent everybody home; and as they went, they said thank you to God for making the boy's little picnic into enough food for thousands of people.

JESUS AND THE SPARROW   *Matthew* 10, 29–31

The Lord Jesus loved all the birds and beasts. One day when He was out He saw some little sparrows. Nobody thought very much of sparrows. If you wanted to buy them you could get two for a farthing. But Jesus loved to see the little birds hopping about, chirruping and fluttering their wings in the dust.

As He was watching them, He saw one fall to the ground. Perhaps it fell out of its nest with a bump. But Jesus knew it would be all right. Our heavenly Father is the Father of the sparrows too, and He knew all about it. He cares for all the little birds, just as He cares for all the boys and girls and all the big people too.

47

BIBLE STORIES

JESUS AND THE BEAUTIFUL FLOWER   *Matthew* 6, 28–9

One day the Lord Jesus went out for a walk in the fields. The sun was shining and the birds were singing, and everything was very beautiful.

Presently the Lord Jesus saw growing in the grass a flower. He stopped and looked at it.

"How beautiful it is," He said. "Look at the lovely colours of its petals. See how soft they are, like satin. Why, this flower is dressed better than the king in his royal robes. How good and kind our Father God must be if He gives the flowers such beautiful clothes to wear!"

HOW JESUS WATCHED HIS MOTHER COOKING   *Matthew* 13, 33

When Jesus was a little boy, He used to watch His mother making bread. First she would take the flour and mix it with water to make a flat dough. It was quite, quite flat. How would it ever grow thick and round, like a loaf or a cake?

Then Jesus' mother, whose name, you know, was Mary, would take a little piece of some stuff called yeast, and mix it in with the dough. Then she would leave it in a warm place. When Jesus went to look at it, the flat dough was all beginning to puff and swell up, or, as we say, to rise. When she had left it long enough, so that it had risen well, Mary would put it in the oven and bake it into nice fresh bread for her little boy's supper.

When Jesus grew up, He told people about the yeast in the bread, and how a tiny bit made all the dough swell up. And so, He said, just a tiny bit of goodness will make everything else good. And we know that one good child in the school or the home helps all the others to be good too.

THE LOST COIN   *Luke* 15, 8–10

Jesus once told a story about a lady who had ten little silver pieces of money, called coins, rather like sixpenny bits. She was very glad to have these little coins, and she kept them very carefully in a safe place.

Then one day, when she was looking at them, one of them fell on the ground and rolled away. She looked everywhere, but she couldn't find it. She was very sad. She went out and talked to her neighbours. "Oh dear," she said, "I have lost one of my coins." And the neighbours were very sorry for her.

Then she went indoors again and had another look. It was dark in her little house, so she took a candle and hunted in all the corners, until at last—she found it! How pleased she was! Out she ran to tell the neighbours. "Be happy with me," she cried, "for I have found the coin I lost." And they were all glad too.

Jesus said our Father God loves all His children as if they were precious coins. And if one of God's children forgets about Him, and strays away, like a lost coin rolling into a dark corner, then God will look and look till He finds that lost child again; and when He has found him, God will be very happy.

THE LOST SHEEP   *Luke* 15, 4–6

There was once a shepherd who had a hundred sheep to look after. Every day he led them to where the grass was sweetest and there was fresh water. And at night he brought them back to the sheepfold, and drove them inside, safe from all wild beasts. Then he counted them to make sure they were all there. And when he was quite sure that none was missing, he lay down across the doorway, for the sheepfold had no door; he himself was the door, and nothing could get past him to harm his sheep.

One day when he counted the sheep, there were only ninety-nine! One was missing. What should he do? Should he stay with the ninety-nine, or should he leave them and go to seek the lost one? That is what he did. He searched and searched (*describe*); till at last he found it. It was so tired and weak with wandering that he had to carry it home on his shoulder; and when he met his neighbours, he cried out to them, "Be happy with me, for I have found my lost sheep." And so he brought it safely home again to the sheepfold. And that, said Jesus, is how God our Father cares for us.

JESUS AND THE LITTLE DONKEY (*For Palm Sunday*)

Mark 11, 1-10

There was once a little donkey, who lived in a village in the land where Jesus was born. He was a very little donkey, and quite young—so young that no one had ever yet ridden on him. He saw other donkeys going by with riders on their backs; but no one had ever ridden him, and he did not think he would like it.

One day he was standing tied up in the village street, when he heard the voices of men coming toward him. They stopped beside him, and one of them said, "This must be the donkey that Jesus told us to bring to Him." They began to untie his rope; but just then his master came out of his house.

"Here," he said, "what are you doing with my donkey?"

"Jesus wants him," said the man who held the rope.

"Oh, if Jesus wants him." said the man, "that's another matter. Take him and welcome."

So the men went off, and the little donkey trotted after them, his hoofs going clip-clop on the hard road. Presently they came to a group of other men who seemed to be waiting for them.

They took the little donkey up to one of these men, who had a wise, kind face. "We found him tied up in the village, Master, just as You told us," they said. This kind man was Jesus.

The little donkey was feeling a bit nervous by this time, with all these strange people. He felt he wanted to run away. But Jesus put out His hand and rubbed his ears, and suddenly the little donkey wasn't afraid any more; he felt quite happy and safe. Even when coats were spread on his back for a saddle, and Jesus was lifted on to it, he didn't mind a bit. He stepped out proudly, and the whole party moved on toward the great city of Jerusalem.

When they came near Jerusalem, the men who were with Jesus began to call out how wonderful He was. And when the people of Jerusalem heard them, they came hurrying up, and they too began to call out, "Blessed is He that cometh in the name of the Lord." They pulled off their clothes and threw them on to the road before the little donkey's feet, and he found himself walking on soft cloth instead of hard ground. That was their way of showing how happy they were that Jesus had come, and of doing Him honour.

The people grew more and more pleased to see Jesus, and more of them came running up to see this wonderful sight. The shouting grew louder and louder; and the people began to pull down branches of trees and strew them on the ground too in front of the little donkey, so that now his hoofs went crunch, crunch. And yet, in spite of all the shouting and waving of branches and the strangeness of it all, the little donkey was quite happy; he had the most wonderful Man in the world on his back, and he just walked proudly on to the end of the journey.

But one thing the little donkey did not know. He did not know that always and always people would remember him, and that every year, when Palm Sunday comes round, we tell the story of the little donkey who carried Jesus on his back as his first rider.

(2) LIST OF OTHER BIBLE STORIES

(Suitable for reading or telling, not including those on pp. 45ff and 80ff.)

INCIDENTS FROM THE LIFE OF JESUS

His birth. Visit of the shepherds.	*Luke*	2,	1–20.
Visit of the wise men.	*Matthew*	2,	1–12.
Flight into Egypt and return.	*Matthew*	2,	13–23.
Jesus in the temple.	*Luke*	2,	40–52.
Healing of the nobleman's son.	*John*	4,	46–53.
Peter's great catch of fish.	*Luke*	5,	1–11.
The man let down through the roof.	*Mark*	2,	1–12.
Healing of ten lepers.	*Luke*	17,	11–19.
Healing of blind Bartimaeus.	*Mark*	10,	46–52.
The raising of Jairus' daughter.	*Mark*	5,	21–24. and 35–43.
Jesus and the children.	*Mark*	10,	13–16.
Jesus calms a storm.	*Mark*	4,	35–41.
The widow's gift.	*Mark*	12,	41–44.
Jesus washes the disciples' feet.	*John*	13,	1–15.
The betrayal.	*Matthew*	26,	47–56.
	Mark	14,	43–50.
	Luke	22,	47–54a.
The condemnation and crucifixion.	*Luke*	23,	13–25. and 33–34.
The resurrection.	*Matthew*	28,	1–10.
	Mark	16,	1–7.
	Luke	24,	1–12.
	John	20,	1–18.
The journey to Emmaus.	*Luke*	24,	13–41.
The ascension.	*Mark*	16,	19–20.
	Luke	24,	50–53.
	Acts	1,	9–11.
The coming of the Holy Spirit.	*Acts*	2,	1–8.

(3) STORIES TO READ

(*These stories depend for their effect on the language, and are not suitable for "telling"*)

The Pig Brother

(*This has been successfully dramatised*)

There was once a child who was untidy. He left his books on the floor, and his muddy shoes on the table; he put his fingers in the jam pots, and spilled ink on his best clothes; there was really no end to his untidiness.

One day the Tidy Angel came into his room.

"This will never do!" said the Angel. "This is really shocking. You must go and stay with your brother while I set things to rights here."

"I have no brother!" said the child.

"Yes, you have," said the Angel. "You may not know him, but he will know you. Go out in the garden and watch for him, and he will soon come."

"I don't know what you mean," said the child; but he went out into the garden and waited.

Presently a squirrel came along, whisking his tail.

53

"Are you my brother?" asked the child.

The squirrel looked him over carefully.

"Well, I should hope not!" he said. "My fur is neat and smooth, my nest is handsomely made, and in perfect order, and my young ones are properly brought up. Why do you insult me by asking such a question?"

He whisked off, and the child waited.

Presently a wren came hopping by.

"Are you my brother?" asked the child.

"No, indeed!" said the wren. "What impertinence! You will find no tidier person than I in the whole garden. Not a feather is out of place, and my eggs are the wonder of all for smoothness and beauty. Brother, indeed!" He hopped off, ruffling his wings, and the child waited.

By and by a large tommy cat came along.

"Are you my brother?" asked the child.

"Go and look at yourself in the glass," said the tommy cat haughtily, "and you will have your answer. I have been washing myself in the sun all morning, while it is plain that no water has come near you for a long time. There are no such creatures as you in my family, I am humbly thankful to say."

He walked on, waving his tail, and the child waited.

Presently a pig came trotting along. The child did not wish to ask if the pig were his brother, but the pig did not wait to be asked.

"Hullo, brother!" he grunted.

"I am not your brother!" said the child.

"Oh yes, you are!" said the pig. "I confess I am not proud of you, but there is no mistaking the members of our family. Come along, and have a good roll in the barnyard! There is some lovely black mud there."

"I don't like to roll in mud!" said the child.

"Tell that to the hens!" said the Pig Brother. "Look at your hands, and your shoes, and your clothes! Come along, I say!

You may have some of the pig-wash for supper, if there is more than I want."

"I don't want pig-wash!" said the child; and he began to cry.

Just then the Tidy Angel came out.

"I have set everything to rights," she said, "and so it must stay. Now, will you go with the Pig Brother, or will you come back with me, and be a tidy child?"

"With you, with you!" cried the child; and he clung to the Angel's dress.

The Pig Brother grunted.

"Small loss!" he said. "There will be all the more wash for me!" And he trotted off.

Laura E. Richards

The Spider's Reward

A Christmas Story

The grey spider ran across the floor of the inn.

"Ugh!" cried the innkeeper's daughter. "Get away, you ugly creature!"

"I wonder if I really am ugly," said the spider to himself, as he climbed up the wall. "Anyway, my web is beautiful." He spun himself a fine big one, and settled in it for the night.

But in the morning, alas! the innkeeper's wife came along with her broom.

"Oh!" she cried. "A cobweb in my clean room!" She swept the beautiful web down, and drove the spider out. "Off you go!" she cried, shooing him with her broom. "I can't bear spiders with their ugly hairy bodies and their horrible long legs."

"Nobody wants me," lamented the poor spider, as he made his way out to the inn stable, and started to spin a web from rafter to rafter. Nobody troubled him there; in fact, the beasts below thanked him for catching the flies which plagued them in the hot weather.

"At least I am useful," said the spider. "If only I were beautiful as well," he added with a sigh.

But since that could not be, he set himself to spin the finest web any spider ever made.

He had been working at it for a long time, when one night there was a great commotion in the stable below—voices and flashing of lights. He could not make out what was happening; but in the morning he looked down and saw in one of the mangers a tiny baby, with a beautiful young woman bending over him while an older man with a kind face stood looking on.

The baby began to cry.

"He is cold," said His mother, "I have covered him with all the straw I can find, but it is not enough."

This was the grey spider's great chance. Down he came from the rafter with his beautiful web, as silken soft as thistledown and as warm as wool, and laid it at the mother's feet. She took it up and laid it over her baby and tucked it snugly round him. He stopped crying and fell happily asleep.

Then Mary, the mother, said to the little grey spider, standing proudly by, "Grey spider, what reward will you take for your lovely gift to my Son?"

"Oh, please," said the spider, clasping his front legs, "if I might only be beautiful!"

"That I cannot do," said Mary. "As the Lord God made you, so you must stay. But I will make people glad to see you, so that if anyone comes across a spider in the evening, he will say, 'Ah, that means good luck!'"

And to this day, in some countries, it is lucky to see a spider in the evening. To this day, too, on Christmas Eve we hang long threads of gold and silver, which we call "angels' hair", on the Christmas tree; and they remind us of the little grey spider, and the gift he gave to the Christ Child on the first Christmas Day.

The Flower that Forgot its Name

When the Lord God first made the world, it was all new. The trees were new, and the birds were new, and the flowers were new; and none of them had any names, because they were so new.

So one day the Lord God began to give everything a name. He named the birds and the beasts, and He gave a name to every flower. When He had finished, He went over them all again to make sure that they knew their names.

All the birds knew their names, and all the beasts knew theirs, and all the flowers too; till at last the Lord God came to a tiny little blue flower.

"Little blue flower," He said kindly, "what name have I given you?"

But the little blue flower couldn't remember. She only hung her head.

"I forget," she whispered.

"Forget *Me* not," said the Lord God.

And ever since then, we have called the tiny blue flower the forget-me-not.

How Saint Francis Wrote a Hymn of the Sun

(from the Canticle of the Sun)

There was once a great and good man called Saint Francis, who loved the birds and the beasts and everything that God had made. He loved them so much that he called them his brothers and sisters.

One day Saint Francis fell very ill. He was a poor man, and the only bedroom he had was a tumble-down hut. As he lay there, the little field-mice ran all over him; and though he loved them, he found it hard, when he was so ill, to have their little feet hurrying and scurrying all over his face. He prayed to God to help him not to mind being so ill, and not being able to drive the mice away.

Then, as he lay there, God began to answer his prayer by putting wonderful thoughts into his mind. These thoughts turned into a hymn of praise to God for all He had made. While he was making it up, Saint Francis forgot all about his illness and the troublesome little mice.

Would you like to hear the hymn that he made? Here it is:

> Praised be my Lord God, with all His creatures; and specially our brother the sun, who brings us the day, and who brings us the light.
> Praised be my Lord for our sister the moon, and for the stars, which He has set clear and lovely in the heaven.
> Praised be my Lord for our brother the wind, and for air and cloud, calms and all weather.
> Praised be my Lord for our sister water, who is very useful to us, and humble and precious and clean.
> Praised be my Lord for our brother fire, through whom Thou givest us light in the darkness; and he is bright and pleasant, and very mighty and strong.
> Praised be my Lord for our mother the earth, which doth hold us and keep us, and bringeth forth fruits, and flowers of many colours, and grass.
> Praise ye and bless ye the Lord, and give thanks unto Him, and serve Him.

Saint Christopher

St. Christopher's special day is June 25th

There was once a man called Offero, who was very big and strong. He was proud of being so strong; and he said to himself, "I am going to find the strongest king in all the world, and serve him."

So he set out, and came to the palace of a great king. With him he took service, and when the king went out to war he fought for him and helped him to conquer his enemies.

But there came a day when the king met a stronger king in battle, and was defeated. Then Offero gave up the service of his first master, and went to serve the new king. And so it went on; he served a king till he found one stronger, and then he served him.

One day, as he sat with the king he was serving in the palace hall, resting after the battle, there came a harper to sing and make music for them. Sweetly the harper sang; but Offero noticed that sometimes he spoke of the Evil One (the devil); and every time he named that name, the king looked afraid and made the sign of the Cross. So Offero knew that his master feared the Evil One; and he left him, and went to seek service with that wicked enemy of all men.

He rode on till he found the Evil One, on a black horse, and said to him, "I have come to be your servant, because you are stronger than all the kings of the world." And the Evil One was glad to have such a strong, brave man. So they rode on together; but as they passed a little hill, they saw on it a Cross, which bore a figure of Jesus Christ. And when he saw it, the Evil One was afraid, and turned to go another way. So Offero knew that Jesus Christ was stronger than the Evil One, and he made up his mind to serve Him only.

He rode on and on, hoping to find Him; but He was nowhere to be found. At last he came to a swiftly flowing river, near which was a cave. In this cave lived a very good man, a hermit. He gave Offero shelter for the night; and the strong man asked him if he knew where Jesus Christ might be found, for he wished to serve Him.

"He is everywhere," said the hermit, "and you can serve Him now. You are as strong as a giant; and you may serve Him here. Many travellers must cross this swift river on foot; and at times they are swept away and drowned. You can carry them on those broad shoulders of yours, so that they cross in safety. And it may be that one day your Master will come to you here."

So Offero joyfully built himself a little hut by the river, and by day and night he carried all travellers over the water. But the years went by, and the Master never came.

Then, one dark, stormy night, Offero thought, "Surely no one will want to cross the river on a night so wild as this"; and he went into his hut to sleep. But in his sleep he heard a gentle knocking at the door, and when he opened it, there stood a little child on the bank.

"Offero, will you carry me across?" he asked.

Offero had never refused to take anyone over; so he lifted the child on his shoulder, grasped his stout staff, and stepped down into the river. But a great storm arose, which tossed the water into rough waves; a mighty wind blew, and the strong current nearly carried him away. As he struggled on, he felt the child on his back growing heavier and heavier, till he began to feel as if he would never gain the other bank of the river.

But at last he touched the shore, worn out and weary, and set the child down. "Never in all my years by the river have I borne across such a heavy burden," said he. "Who may you be, little stranger?"

As he spoke, the storm ceased, and a light shone round the little child. Then Offero knew that he had carried on his shoulders the Christ child, the baby Jesus, the Lord of all the world. He knelt down, and heard a voice saying to him, "All these years by the river, as you carried the folk across, you have been serving Me. Your name shall no longer be Offero, but Christ-offero, Christopher, the Christ-bearer."

Then the strong man knew that he had found the strongest King in all the world; and he served him joyously all the rest of his days.

(4) STORIES OF BIRDS AND BEASTS—to read or tell

These stories are mostly legends of the saints, illustrating simple themes such as the love of God; His care for His creation, both man and beast; the tenderness for animals which He puts into the hearts of those who love Him. The stories are purposely given only in simple outline, since the story-teller will probably prefer to tell them from memory, adding such detail at the time as heightens the effect.

The events all happened in the very early days of the Christian era, during the fifth and sixth centuries A.D., and the background to most of them is wild, trackless country inhabited by peasant folk with a simple culture such as is found today in some parts of western Ireland, but with no background of civilisation and no means of transport other than on foot, or by horse, ass or boat. In such a setting the imagination can be given free rein, in filling in the natural background to the stories.

The children will readily appreciate the idea that a saint is a good man who loves God and does what pleases Him.

Saint Cadoc and the Mouse

Saint Cadoc's special day is January 24th

Long ago, in the mountains of Wales, there lived a boy called Cadoc. Cadoc loved God very much; and he wanted to be able to tell other people about Him too. So one day he came down from the mountains to a village in the valley, where there lived a holy man who could teach him how to do that.

But when he came to the village, he found everyone very sad. There had been bad weather, and the people had not been able to harvest enough hay and corn to last them through the winter. Soon it would be gone, and then they must go hungry. So when Cadoc went to the holy man and asked to be allowed to stay in the village and learn to be a teacher, he shook his head.

"There is no food for you here, my son," he said. "We are praying to God that we may not all starve this winter."

Cadoc was very disappointed. He went away and sat down under a tree to see what to do next. As he sat there, he heard a rustling, and looking down he saw a little mouse coming out of a hole, and in its mouth it carried a grain of wheat. It ran away, and presently came back without the grain, and went into the hole again. Again it came out with a grain of wheat in its mouth, and ran away with it to put it in its winter store. Cadoc sat watching while the little mouse went again and again. Suddenly the boy said to himself, "Where is the mouse getting all this grain? Can there be a storehouse hidden under the earth?"

Very gently he caught the mouse, and tied a white thread from his coat round it. Then he let it go again, and it scuttled away. Cadoc followed it, keeping his eyes on the white thread; and at last he saw it disappear into the side of a hill. Cadoc fetched men with spades, and they dug into the hillside; and in time they came to an old cellar, belonging to a house which had stood there long before. It had fallen in ruins, and the earth had covered it up; but in the cellar there were still sacks of corn, enough to feed the hungry people all through the winter and to sow in the fields in the spring. So Cadoc was able to stay in the village, and learn from the holy man; then he went back to his mountains and taught the people there; and they loved him so much, and he was such a good man, that he was called Saint Cadoc.

Saint Cuthbert and the Eagle

Saint Cuthbert's special day is March 20th

Long ago, in Scotland, there lived a very good man called Saint Cuthbert. One day the people in a far-away village sent to ask him to come and tell them about God; and they sent a boy called Cedda to show him the way through the wild country; for there were no roads in those far-off days.

They had hoped to reach Cedda's village in the afternoon; but somehow they lost their way, and Saint Cuthbert said to Cedda, "I fear we shall not reach the village to-night. Is there any house or hut near by where we can find shelter and food?"

"There are some huts," said the boy. "But the people who live in them are very poor, and they will not have food for us." Poor Cedda! He did not at all like the idea of having no supper.

"God is our loving Father, Cedda," said Cuthbert. "I am sure He will give us all we need. Let us pray to Him and ask Him for help." So they prayed, and then journeyed on.

Presently they saw wheeling in the air a great bird.

"Look," said Cedda. "An eagle, hunting for food!"

Suddenly the eagle swooped down to earth as if it had seen something to eat.

"Run and see what he has caught," said Cuthbert. "Perhaps this is God's way of answering our prayer."

Down below them lay a river; and the boy ran down the hill to its bank. There stood the eagle, struggling with a great salmon which it had caught. When it saw the boy and the man, it tried to rise in the air with its prey and fly away; but the fish was so big and heavy that the bird was obliged to let it fall.

Cedda ran and picked it up. "Here is our supper," he cried.

But Cuthbert looked up at the eagle, still wheeling above and watching with angry eyes those who had stolen his meal.

"We must give the bird his share," he said. "God sent him to us, and we must feed him."

So they divided the fish, and left a large piece for the bird. Then, carrying the rest, they went joyfully on their way. And Cedda thought that Cuthbert must have learnt from God Himself how to care for all creatures, even the fierce eagle.

Saint Jerome and the Lion

Saint Jerome's special day is September 30th

Saint Jerome was a very good man, who lived with his friends in a big house called a monastery.

One day he was sitting at the monastery door when he saw coming toward him a big lion. All his friends ran away in terror at the sight; but Jerome waited quietly. The lion came up to him, looked into his kind face, and lifted up its paw. Jerome looked at it, and saw that it was swollen, and that the poor lion must be in great pain. He took the paw in his hand, and saw that there was a big thorn sticking out of the pad. Very gently he took hold of the thorn and pulled it out. Then he took the lion indoors, washed the sore paw, and bandaged it up.

Then he tried to make the lion go away. But it lay down at his feet, and refused to go. It was so grateful to this kind man who had taken away the pain that it wanted to stay with him.

So Jerome left the lion and went to bed; and in the morning he found the beast still there. Again he tried to send it away, but it would not go.

"Everyone works in a monastery," said Saint Jerome. "If you stay with us, you must work too. You must go every day with my donkey, when the old woodcutter drives him out to get firewood; and while the woodcutter chops the wood and loads the donkey, you must keep guard over them and see that no harm comes to them."

So every day the lion went out into the forest with the donkey and the woodcutter, and guarded them against robbers. But one day it was so very hot and quiet, there under the trees, that the lion fell fast asleep. When he awoke, there was no donkey and no woodcutter! He smelt the smell of men, and knew that robbers must have taken them.

Sadly he went back to the monastery; and when Jerome saw him without the donkey, and looking so ashamed of himself, he said sternly, "So you have not done your duty! Then you must take the donkey's place, and go for firewood."

So every day the lion went into the forest and was loaded with wood to carry home; and he bore it patiently. Then one day there passed by a company of merchants, with a long line of horses and camels, loaded with fine things; and at the head of the line was a donkey led by an old man.

The lion looked at them and sniffed the air: then suddenly, with a great roar, he sprang toward them, for he had recognised his master's stolen donkey. The merchants fled in terror; and the lion, roaring after them, drove them all to the monastery. Jerome came out to see what this strange sight could mean —horses, camels, donkey and men all crowding into the courtyard. Then the merchants confessed that they had stolen the donkey, and begged Jerome to forgive them. And he, overjoyed at having his donkey back, forgave them gladly. So once again Jerome's two faithful servants, the donkey and the lion, went to the forest for firewood; and the lion stayed with the saint till the end of his days.

Saint Felix and the Spider

Saint Felix's special day is October 12th

There was once a good man called Saint Felix, who lived in Italy, in a city called Rome. The Emperor of Rome was very angry with Saint Felix because he was a Christian; and he shut him up in a dark prison. There Saint Felix had to stay for a long time; and he was given so little to eat that he grew very, very thin.

Then, one day, God showed him how to escape from his prison; and he ran right away from Rome. But the Emperor's soldiers rode after him on swift horses; and though he ran his fastest, he knew that they would soon catch him up and take him back to prison again.

He ran and ran, and presently he came to a valley which lay between high mountains. On either side were nothing but hard rocks; and Saint Felix thought to himself that now he must surely be caught; he could not climb the mountains, and there was no place to hide in the rocks.

But just then he saw a narrow crack in one of the rocks, and he said to himself, "Since I am so thin, perhaps I could squeeze through there." So he tried; and he just managed to get through. On the other side of the crack there was a deep, dry well; and Saint Felix scrambled down into it and thought that perhaps now he would be safe.

But presently he heard the sound of horses' hooves, and knew that the soldiers were looking for him in the valley.

"Where can he have got to?" said one of them.

"Look," said another, "here is a crack in the rock—perhaps he is through there. I am going to see."

Poor Saint Felix felt his heart go bump, bump. But then he heard another soldier say, "No, he can't be there—look, there's a spider's web across it. No one has gone that way." And the soldiers rode on.

Then Saint Felix knew that in some wonderful way God must have sent a spider to spin a web across the crack and save his life, and he said a "thank you" prayer to Him. He stayed in the dry well for a long time, and kind friends brought him food. But at last it was safe for him to go home again to his family and friends; and he told them of his escape and asked them always to be kind to spiders.

Saint Neot and the Rooks

Saint Neot's special day is October 28th

There was once a good man called Saint Neot. He was quite a little man; but he had a very big, kind heart. He loved God very much, and he wanted to tell people all about Him, so that they would love Him too.

One day Saint Neot came to a land called Cornwall, where in those days people did not know anything about God. So he took a little bell, and walked about ringing it; and when all the people came, he said, "Stay here and listen, for I want to tell you about God, your loving heavenly Father."

But the people were farmers, and they said, "No, no, we cannot stay and listen; for we have just sown our seed, and if we do not watch it, the rooks will come and peck it out of the ground. Then we shall have no wheat to make bread; and if we have no bread, we shall be hungry. No, we cannot stay and listen."

At first Saint Neot was very sad; but then, because he was a good man, God spoke to him and told him what to do. He went along till he came to the tall trees where the rooks had their nests, and he rang his little bell again. Down flew all the rooks and settled on the ground round Saint Neot; and he told them what he wanted them to do.

Then the rooks flew up in the air again, and they circled round and round, and then down they all came in one place, a square little place where once a Roman camp had been. And there they sat, cawing away busily, but not moving at all.

Then Saint Neot rang his bell again; and when the people came out of their farms, he said, "Look, all the rooks are gathered in one place, and there they have promised me that they will stay till I have finished talking to you about God your heavenly Father." And when the people saw what had happened, they felt that they must come and listen to this kind little man who could talk to the rooks and make them do what he asked. So they sat round him, just as the rooks had done, and he told them about God; and they all became different people, not greedy or unkind or selfish any more; and everyone in the land of Cornwall was happy. And whenever Saint Neot wanted to talk to the people, he always talked to the rooks first, and they went and sat in the Roman camp again.

Perhaps one of the things Saint Neot told his people was that the rooks do not really take the corn out of the ground; they are the farmer's friends, who eat up the insects which might spoil the corn. So if you see rooks hopping about in a cornfield, you can think of Saint Neot and his rook friends long ago.

Saint Malo and the Wrens

Saint Malo's day is November 15th

Long ago, in the land of Brittany, in France, there lived a good man called Saint Malo. He lived by the sea and there he built himself a tiny little house with only one room in it.

Outside his tiny house, Saint Malo made himself a little garden, and in the springtime it was gay with sweet-smelling flowers. He loved his little garden, and every day he worked hard in it. One day he worked so hard that he grew hot, and took off the hood of his long brown robe, which he wore in cold weather. It was just like the hoods that some people wear on their mackintoshes. He hung it up on a tree and went on with his gardening.

Now it happened that two little wrens were looking for a nesting place. There were not many good places down there by the sea shore, and they were flying about looking everywhere. As they flew by, the mother bird saw the hood hanging there, and into it she flew. It seemed to her just the right place for a cosy nest; so off she went with the father bird to gather twigs and nice soft material to build it. In and out they flew; and all the time Saint Malo went on working, and never saw at all what they were doing.

At last the nest was made, and mother bird flew in and found it just to her liking. She settled down and laid a tiny egg, and sat there keeping it warm. But by this time it was evening, a cool breeze was blowing from the sea, and Saint Malo wanted his hood. He took it down from the tree—and what was his surprise when out flew a little bird. He guessed at once what had happened. He put in his hand, and found the soft little nest, and felt the tiny egg. The poor mother bird was flying round and round in great distress—what was this great creature going to do with her little home?

Saint Malo loved animals and birds as well as flowers; and he just hung the hood up on the branch again, and went indoors without it. The mother bird waited a bit, then, when she saw that all was quiet, back she came, and settled down once more. She laid more eggs, and then began to hatch them. All day long she sat there, and day after day, while the father bird brought her tasty titbits. And all the time, even when the wind blew chill, Saint Malo had no cosy hood.

But he would not disturb the little birds. He watched them till the eggs hatched, and father and mother bird flew back and forth all day long feeding the hungry babies. At last they were big enough to fly, and one day they all flew away out into the big world. And only then did the good Saint Malo take his hood back again.

Saint Leonore and the Robin

(It has not been possible to find a special date for this story; but it could be used either for spring or autumn, and would be very suitable for a Harvest Assembly)

There was once a good man called Saint Leonore, who lived with his friends in a big house called a monastery. The country where they lived was very beautiful, and all around the monastery there were woods and grassy meadows and fields full of golden corn and ponds with fine fish in them. In the monastery there was always plenty to eat—fish from the ponds and honey from the bees, and bread from the golden corn.

Leonore and his friends were very happy, for they loved God and looked after each other.

But one day news came to the monastery that in a land across the sea lived poor people who did not know of God, their loving Father, but fought and killed each other. "We must go to them," said Leonore to his friends, "and tell them about God." And his friends said they would go with him.

So they took a ship; and with them they took all they would need in the new land—food and clothes and tools to build houses with, and plenty of corn to plant, so that they could grind it into flour and make bread. But on the way there was a great storm, and though Leonore and his friends came safe to land, all the things they had brought went to the bottom of the sea.

They built themselves a hut in the new land, and lived as best they could on nuts and berries and whatever animals or fish they could catch. They met the people of the land, too, and found how poor they were. "If only," said Leonore, "we had some corn to plant, we could give these poor folk bread. But we can only just manage to feed ourselves and we have no food to spare for them." And he thought sadly of the great cornfields round the monastery at home.

Then one day, as Leonore was praying, it seemed to him as if God spoke to him, and promised to send the corn to plant if he and his friends would make ready for it. So Leonore said to the other men, "Let us make a field for sowing." Perhaps they thought this a strange thing to do, when there was no seed to sow; but they did as Leonore asked them. They cleared a piece of ground, and ploughed the earth, and fenced it round with a stone wall. Then they prayed to God to send the seed, and waited to see what would happen.

Just then overhead flew a little robin, with a long straw in his beak; and he let it fall at Leonore's feet. He picked it up, and there on the end of it was a whole big ear of wheat, filled with golden grains. Joyfully he and his friends picked them all out, and planted them one by one in the tiny field they had made ready. They tended them carefully, and in time there were many more wheat stalks, each with its head of grain. Again these grains were planted, and in time there was enough wheat to make bread, and nobody need go hungry any more. Then Leonore and his friends sang praises to God, for sending the little robin to bring His people their daily bread.

Saint Francis and the Wolf

St. Francis's special day is October 4th

There was once a good man called Saint Francis, who was so good and kind that everyone loved him, even the birds and the beasts.

One day as he was travelling, he came to a town where he found everyone very frightened. A fierce wolf lived in the forest near by and attacked those who went out of the town, so that the people were afraid to go anywhere.

"I will go and talk to Brother Wolf," said Francis. But the people begged him not to go. "You will be killed," they said.

But Francis was not afraid. He went out of the town toward the place where the wolf lived, and the wolf came bounding out, ready to spring upon him. But Francis spoke gently to it; and when the wolf heard his voice, it became quiet, and came and bent its head to the ground in front of Francis. Then he talked to it, and told it that it had been very wicked, to hurt and frighten the poor people; and the wolf showed as well as it could that it was sorry.

"Will you come back with me to the town," asked Francis, "and tell the people there that you are sorry?" And the wolf bowed its head to show that it would. Then Francis led it to the market place, and all the people came crowding round to see the wonderful sight. And again Francis asked the wolf if it were sorry; and again the wolf showed by signs that it was.

71

"Brother Wolf," said Francis, "I know that you did this wrong because you were hungry, and wanted food. But now, if I ask the townspeople to feed you, so that you are not hungry any more, will you promise not to do them any hurt?" And the wolf, by signs, showed that it promised.

After that, the wolf went around with Francis like a faithful dog; and the townsfolk fed it, and let it walk in and out of their houses. It did no one any harm; and when at last it grew old and died, the people were really sad to lose their favourite, Brother Wolf.

Saint Francis and the Swallows

One day that very good man called Saint Francis, who loved all the birds and the beasts, was walking along with some of his friends, when they came to a place with a wall round it, like a garden.

"This would be a good place," said Saint Francis, "to stop and tell the people about God our loving heavenly Father."

So they went into the walled place; and when all the people who lived near by heard that they were there, they came flocking to hear what they had to say; for everyone loved Saint Francis and his friends.

So Saint Francis began to speak to them; but in the trees all round them were many swallows making their nests, and they made such a twittering that nobody could hear what he said.

Saint Francis looked up to where the birds were perched.

"My little brothers the swallows," he said, "please be quiet while I am speaking." And to the astonishment of all who were there, the birds at once ceased their twittering, and not another sound did they make till Saint Francis had finished speaking. When he had done, the good man went on his way; but first, you may be sure, he thanked his little brothers, the swallows, who had helped him in his work.

Saint Francis and the Birds

One day the good Saint Francis and his friends came to a place where there were many trees; and in the trees they saw multitudes of birds, of all the kinds you can possibly imagine. Saint Francis looked at them, and thought how beautiful they were, and how wonderful it was that each little bird should be so different from its neighbour.

Then he said to the friends who were with him, "You wait here on the road—I am going to speak to the birds my sisters." For Saint Francis loved all the birds and the beasts so much that he often spoke of them as his brothers and sisters.

Saint Francis's friends were very surprised to hear him say he was going to talk to the birds; but they were still more surprised when he went into the field where they were, and began to talk to a few birds which were hopping about on the ground. For presently down flew the birds which were in the trees, and settled on the ground all round him; and then he began to talk to them, just as if they were people.

"My sisters the birds," he said, "you ought to thank God, who made you, very much, always and wherever you are. He lets you fly wherever you like, and gives you lovely thick warm feathers for clothes. There are safe places for you in the mountains and valleys, and high trees in which you can build your nests. And because you cannot sew or spin, He dresses you and your babies Himself. You see how much He loves you, because He gives you so many good things. And so, my sisters the birds, you must always remember to say thank you to Him, and praise Him for His goodness."

Then the friends who were watching saw that while Saint Francis was speaking to them, all the birds began to open their beaks and stretch out their necks and flutter their wings and bow their heads to the ground, to show how happy they were to see Saint Francis and to hear him talking. And Saint Francis was very happy too, and he was astonished that they listened to him so quietly and were not at all afraid of him, not even when he moved among them and his cloak brushed against them as he passed.

At last, when he had finished speaking to them, Saint Francis made over them the sign of the Cross, and told them they might go; and then all that great crowd of birds rose into the air, singing with all their might, and flew out of sight.

How the Ox and the Ass kept Christmas

A Christmas Story of Saint Francis

Long, long ago, about Christmas time, a little man was driving an ox and an ass up a steep mountain side. He wore a long brown coat, or robe, with a cord tied round his waist; and as he drove the beasts up the steep pathway, he was not shouting at them, as people usually do when they drive cattle; he was saying, "Come along now, Brother Ox!", and "Up you go, little Brother Ass."

Who was this little man? And why did he call the beasts his brothers? And where was he taking them that day so long ago? His name was Francis; and because he was such a good man, people called him Saint Francis. Saint Francis loved everything and everyone. He loved the birds and the beasts so much that he called them his brothers and sisters; he loved the people, even the cross ones; and most of all he loved God.

When Christmas time came, and he thought about Baby Jesus, he loved Him so much that he kept talking to everyone about Him, and about the stable where He was born, and about Mary His mother, and Joseph, and the beasts who stood by the manger where He lay. He could see it all so plainly. But the other people couldn't. They couldn't think what it must have been like. One day, when Francis was staying in a big house on top of a mountain, he found a cave in the mountain side, which seemed to him exactly like the stable where Baby Jesus was born; and he said to himself, "Now I'll *show* them what it was like."

So he sent out messages to all his friends in the mountain villages and down in the valleys, inviting them to come to the cave at night and see something very special. "What could it be?" they wondered; but everyone loved Saint Francis, so they all said they would come.

Then Francis went down the mountain, and paid some visits. First he went to see a man and woman he knew, and told them what he wanted them to do. You will hear what it was presently. Then he went on to see a friend who had an ox.

"Friend," he said, "may I borrow your ox till tonight, for something very special?" And because the friend loved Francis, he said yes. So Francis went on, driving the ox before him, till he came to the house of another friend, who had a little donkey.

"Friend," he said, "may I borrow your little donkey till tonight for something very special?" And because the friend loved Francis, he said yes. So Francis went on again, driving before him the ox and the ass. All the long way up the mountain he drove them, and into the cave at the top.

That evening all the neighbours came out of their homes, and began to climb the mountain. They all carried torches, so as to be able to see their way. If you had stood in the valley and looked up, you would have seen little twinkling lights everywhere, going up and up the mountain paths right to the very top. When the people reached the cave, there was a light shining out of it; and when they looked in, what do you think they saw?

There were the ox and the ass standing by a manger; and there was a lady sitting beside it, and a man looking on. And the people whispered to each other, "Look! There is Mary, and there is Joseph, and there are the ox and the ass; and in the manger there must be Baby Jesus. *Now* we know just what it was like, because we have seen it for ourselves."

So that was the Christmas surprise which Saint Francis gave to his friends; and that was how the ox and the ass kept Christmas.

Section 7

Dramatic Hints

on

BIBLE STORIES SUITABLE FOR ACTING

A number of teachers report that when they are taking small classes for ·Assembly, or when there is an extended Assembly, such as is described on p. 88, it is often possible to dramatise a Bible story. Below are given a number of outlines which may be useful in picking out a story to tell and dramatise. All give plenty of scope for non-speaking parts, both human—disciples, soldiers, attendants, harvesters, etc.— and animal—sheep, camels, pigs, lions, and all the beasts which went into the ark, which allow full scope to the imagination.

The words in italics denote the characters in each story.

I. ADAM AND EVE   *Genesis 3*

Eve in the garden with the *Serpent*. She is led astray by his arguments and eats an apple. *Adam* enters, is tempted by Eve and falls. The voice of *God* is heard rebuking them, and telling them that they must leave Eden and work for their living. Sorrowfully they depart.

2. NOAH AND THE ARK   *Genesis 6, 9—9, 17*

The voice of *God* tells *Noah* of His intending punishment of mankind, and tells him to build the ark. He calls his *three sons* and tells them of the plan. They start to build. The *neighbours* inquire and laugh. The rain threatens, and the *animals* are driven two by two into the ark. The rain begins, and continues for forty days. Noah, looking out of the window, gives a commentary. He sees the waters sinking, and sends out a *raven*, which returns. He sends a *dove*, which returns with an olive branch. He sends her out again, and she does not return. The ark grounds on Mount Ararat, and the animals emerge again two by two. God's voice promises that the seasons shall continue normally; the rainbow is seen.

3. THE FINDING OF REBEKAH   *Genesis* 24

Abraham summons his *servant Eliezer* and sends him to find a wife for his son Isaac among his own people. Eliezer departs with *camels* and *servants*. He comes to the well, and prays that the girl who gives him and his camels drink will be the wife for Isaac. *Rebekah* comes and draws water for them. She takes them home, and agrees to become Isaac's wife. The party leave, and are met on their return by *Isaac*, who welcomes Rebekah as his wife.

4. JOSEPH   *Genesis* 37, 3–45, end

It is impossible to give an outline of this epic. The teacher will know what to select.

5. MOSES, THE RIVER BABY   *Exodus* 1, 22–2, 10

Moses' parents with *Miriam* and *Aaron* and the baby (a doll); they discuss Pharaoh's edict and how to save Moses; they decide to make a floating cradle. It is made and placed in the water. Then *Pharaoh's daughter* and her *maidens* come to bathe, and see it. They find the child and the princess decides to adopt him. Miriam fetches her mother as a foster-mother. When *Moses* is a small boy, his mother brings him to the palace to be brought up as the princess's son.

6. RUTH   *Ruth*

Elimelech takes his wife *Naomi* and his *two sons* to Moab to escape famine in Judah. The next scene shows Naomi, now a widow, telling her *daughters-in-law*, who have also lost their husbands, that she is returning to Judah. They set out, and after a time Naomi bids them go back; Orpah takes an affectionate farewell; but Ruth goes with her to Judah. Ruth proposes to go gleaning; and works in the field of *Boaz*. He inquires who she is, and having heard of her goodness to Naomi, gives orders to the *harvesters* that she is to be given the best treatment. She returns to Naomi with what she has gleaned, and Naomi tells her that Boaz is a kinsman. Boaz decides to marry Ruth.

7. SAMUEL   1 *Samuel* 1 *and* 3

A happy *family party*. *Hannah* sits silent in grief for her childlessness. She goes to the temple and prays, promising to give her child to God. (*Eli's* misunderstanding may be omitted if too difficult.) He blesses her. She returns to him later, bringing *Samuel*. Samuel learns his work. He goes to bed, and wakes to hear *a voice* calling him. Three times he goes to Eli; the third time Eli tells him it is the voice of God. (For small children the story can end at Samuel's response to God; older children could put in God's message to Eli through Samuel, and how he gave it to Eli next morning—1 *Samuel* 3, 11–18.)

8. DAVID IS ANOINTED KING   1 *Samuel* 16, 1–13

God orders *Samuel* to go to Bethlehem and anoint as king one of the sons of *Jesse*. Jesse produces *seven sons*, in vain. He mentions the youngest, David, who is out with the sheep, and Samuel orders him to be sent for. A *messenger* comes to *David* among the *sheep*. He returns, and is anointed by Samuel as king.

9. DAVID AND GOLIATH   1 *Samuel* 17

David arrives in camp with food for his *brothers*. He is talking to them when the *Philistine giant* begins to shout a challenge to the armies of Israel. No one answers. David offers to fight him, and is taken to *King Saul* who offers him armour. But David tells how he has slain a lion and a bear unarmed, and goes to meet Goliath. He slings a stone, and the giant falls dead. David is acclaimed as a hero by the *Israelites*.

10. ELIJAH AND THE RAVENS   I *Kings* 17, 1–16

God tells *Elijah* he is in danger, and must hide by the brook Cherith, drinking from it and fed by *ravens*. He goes there, and the ravens bring him food. After a time the brook dries up, and the voice of God tells Elijah to go to Zarephath, where a *widow* will feed him. He reaches the city, and meets her gathering firewood. He begs a drink of water and food. She says she has only a little meal and oil. He tells her that it will suffice for her, her *son* and himself till the Lord sends rain. She takes him home and they have a meal.

11. NAAMAN AND THE LITTLE SLAVE GIRL   2 *Kings* 5, 1–16, 19

The *little captive*, with other *servants*, is in attendance on *Naaman's wife*, who speaks sadly of his leprosy. She says she is sure the prophet Elisha could cure him. A servant tells *Naaman*, who reports it to the *King of Syria*. The king sends him to find the prophet. He arrives at the house of *Elisha*, who sends out a message that he is to dip seven times in Jordan. Naaman, outraged, departs; but *his men* reason with him and he bathes and is cured. He returns to Elisha, full of gratitude, and offering gifts, which he refuses, dismissing him with, "Go in peace."

12. DANIEL AT COURT   *Daniel* 1, 1–20

Daniel and his *three friends* are in the slave market in Babylon. A *royal chamberlain* comes seeking boys to be trained as courtiers, and buys the four friends. He gives them court clothing and tells them they will be given the best palace food to fit them for their post. Daniel says that by their religion he and his friends may not have that food, and suggests a simple diet. The chamberlain is afraid they will not be so well under it as the rest, but Daniel begs him to try. When they are brought before the *king*, he chooses them as his personal attendants.

13. DANIEL'S FRIENDS IN THE FURNACE   *Daniel* 3

The *king* decrees the setting up of an idol to be worshipped by all the people. *Enemies* report that Daniel's *three friends* are disobeying the edict. They are brought before the king, and refuse to obey. He orders them to be thrown into the furnace. This is done by *soldiers*, who are killed by its heat. The king starts up, seeing four men in the fire, the fourth like an *angel*. He calls the three out and they emerge unhurt, saying God has preserved them. The king praises God and promotes the three.

14. DANIEL IN THE DEN OF LIONS   *Daniel 6*

The *king* issues an edict that all must worship him. *Enemies* report that *Daniel* is disobeying by worshipping God. He is condemned and cast into the den of *lions*. The king cannot sleep, and rising early, goes to the den and calls to Daniel, who replies that God has kept him safe. Punishment of enemies—God glorified.

NEW TESTAMENT

15. THE NATIVITY   *Matthew* 2, 1–12; *Luke* 2, 1–20

There is no need to give an outline for this story; every school has its own nativity play.

16. ZACCHAEUS, THE LITTLE MAN WHO WANTED TO SEE JESUS
Luke 19, 1–10

Zacchaeus goes along the street, followed by jeers for his smallness and curses from *those* he has robbed and cheated. *Someone* says Jesus is coming, and *all* crowd to the roadside. Zacchaeus tries to make a way through to see for himself, but he cannot. No one will make way. He climbs a sycamore tree, and there is more jeering. *Jesus* passes, stops and asks him to come down and give Him and His *disciples* dinner. *People* protest; and Zacchaeus declares that he will restore fourfold. They all go on to the dinner, at which Jesus says, "Today salvation has come to this house." (*Explain*.)

17. HEALING OF THE NOBLEMAN'S SON   *John 4, 46–53*

Boy ill in bed. Anxious *parents*, *doctor*, helpless. *Someone* mentions *Jesus*. Father sets out to find Him. He meets Him, and begs Him to help. Jesus demurs; the father pleads again. Jesus says, "Go home; your son is alive." He sets out, and is met by his *servants* with the good news. He asks the time of the recovery, and realises that it was when Jesus gave His promise, and declares that he will follow Him with all his household.

18. THE FEEDING OF THE FIVE THOUSAND   *John 6, 3–14*

Jesus preaching to a large *crowd*. He asks His *disciples* how they can be fed. *Philip* says it would need seven pounds' worth of bread. *Andrew* brings up the *boy* with five loaves and two fish. Jesus makes the people sit down, breaks the bread and fish and gives it to the disciples to distribute. All eat, and Jesus orders the pieces to be gathered up, which is done.

19. EASTER MORNING   *John 20, 1–18*

Peter and *John* sitting sadly grieving over the death of Jesus. *Mary* runs in with the news that the tomb is empty. They run to it; John gets there first and looks in, Peter goes in. They are puzzled, and go home. Mary has followed them, and stands sobbing by the tomb. She sees *two angels* who ask her why she weeps. She explains, then turns and sees *Jesus*. He too asks her why she weeps, and whom she seeks. She begs to know where the body is. Jesus calls her by name, and she recognises Him. He gives her a message for the *disciples*, and she runs to tell them He is risen.

PARABLES

20. THE GOOD SAMARITAN   *Luke 10, 30–35*

Robbers attack a *traveller*, and leave him lying wounded. *Priest* and *Levite* pass by; *Samaritan* tends his wounds, takes him to an inn on his *ass*, leaves him in the care of the *innkeeper*, with money for his expenses, and promises to foot the bill if need be.

21. THE LOST SHEEP   *Luke* 15, 4–6

Shepherd drives into the fold his *sheep*. He counts them and finds that *one* is missing. He sets out to find it, searches everywhere, finds it, and brings it home. He rejoices with *neighbours* whom he passes on the way.

22. THE LOST COIN   *Luke* 15, 8–10

Woman counting coins finds one is missing. She searches everywhere in vain; then lights a candle, and seeks in corners. At last she finds it, and gathers her *friends* and *neighbours* to rejoice with her.

23. THE PRODIGAL SON   *Luke* 15, 11–24 or 32

Father with *two sons*—younger asks for his share of the estate, and departs. He spends his money in riotous *parties* (act one in progress), but one day finds his money bag empty, and himself in want. He hires himself out to herd *pigs*; then he comes to his senses and determines to go home and serve his father. He sets out, and is met by his father, who orders the *servants* to give him the best clothing and food. (The behaviour of the *elder brother* may be a little perplexing for the small children; but the older ones will understand it and be happy to act it.)

Section 8

Teachers' Own Suggestions and Experiences

As with the *Junior Assembly Book*, teachers have very generously given of their best to help build up this section, which in the previous volume was found to be of especial value. Those who have contributed are of varying types—headmistresses who have the whole school for Assembly, assistant teachers in charge of one or more classes, who take a smaller assembly with them, and those teaching in quite small schools. In this way it is hoped that the needs of all will be met.

(A) HINTS AND SUGGESTIONS

1. Celebrating birthdays.

(*a*) "Birthday children come to the front. We say a greeting, and sing 'Happy, happy birthday'. After Assembly, the child comes up to my room for a birthday card. I keep a stock of old ones for this purpose, with labels pasted over the original greetings."

(*b*) "On Thursdays we remember children who have had birthdays during the week. The birthday children stand in front and each lights a candle. These are Christmas tree candles, stuck into a wooden holder an inch thick and fifteen inches long, with five holes bored in it to take the candles. Then we all say, 'We wish you many happy returns of the day.' Then a child is chosen to give each birthday child a sweet, handing them round in a saucer. There is a reminder of politeness in the 'thank you's'. The children eat the sweets while we stand and sing, 'Comes a birthday once again'. Then the birthday children blow out the candles. This idea of lighting candles and having sweets certainly helps new children to feel happy, and part of the family in the class."

(c) "The headmistress says, 'All birthday children come here'. All line up. We have a model birthday cake, and the class teacher lights five, six or seven candles on it, for each child respectively. Meanwhile the headmistress looks at the birthday cards which the child has received and brought to school, and makes comments on them. Then comes the moment to blow out the candles, while the children, sitting on the floor, clap heartily. The birthday children then stand in front of the table, and we all sing,

> Happy birthday to you,
> Happy birthday to you,
> Happy birthday, dear children,
> Happy birthday to you."

2. The inclusion of parents.

"On Wednesday, when the whole school, Nursery and Infants together, have a joint Assembly lasting about twenty minutes, it is our custom to invite parents to be present. As most of them work, we usually get mothers with babies and toddlers; but fathers sometimes come, and grandmothers too appreciate the opportunity to join us.

"We begin with a sung introit, greetings are exchanged, and there is a hymn sung by the children, and usually practised the previous week. Then there is a reading, by one of the top class Infants, chosen and practised during the week by the class teacher. This is varied sometimes by a poem.

"The reading is followed by the Mothers' Hymn, chosen from the School Hymn Book by the mother of the child who reads the lesson, and sung by the parents present alone.

"Any birthdays are then celebrated, and the children march out to music. The whole Assembly is a family affair. Often at the end the nursery children wave good-bye, first to the head-mistress, then to mothers and friends. Sometimes the mothers stay behind to hear special news from the headmistress, or to chat with her over some special problem connected with their children."

3. The use of silence.

An increasing number of teachers find that a very brief time of silence, at the beginning, the middle or the end of Assembly, has a very real effect on small children. Specific instances of how it helps will be found in the "teachers' experiences" which follow. When one remembers the homes from which some children come, and the atmosphere which prevails there, and remembers too the sensitiveness to everything of a small child, it is clearly unreasonable to expect peace and concentration without such an aid. Sometimes the story of Samuel (1 *Samuel* 3) or some other "listening" story leads naturally to a time of quiet.

But it is important that such silence should be purposive, and the children should have some idea of its aim and content. Teachers who habitually use silence generally preface it by some such phrase as:

"Let us be quiet, and remember that God is here with us."
"Let us be quiet and think what news we have to tell."
"Let us think quietly what we want to ask God for today."

Sometimes the theme is more specific:

"Let us think of our mothers, and thank God for them."
"Let us think how we can be helpful today."
"Let us think about all sick children, especially . . . and ask God to make them well."
"Let us think of the nicest thing we have, and thank God for it."
"Let us thank God for Baby Jesus."
"Let us think if we have done anything wrong, and tell God

we are sorry, and ask Him to help us to do better next time."

In some schools, as in the one whose Assembly is described on pages 93–5, teacher and children listen specifically for the voice of God, and afterwards tell each other the thoughts which have come into their minds. From another school comes the following list of some of the thoughts which came to the children during the silence, and which they themselves wrote down in large letters on small pieces of paper (with their own spelling):

"Jesus said He would give us all a very happy day."

"Miss N. will help the children to do the best."

"You did well at the baths, but not at your sums."

"Do not speak when anybody else is speaking."

"You will have all your money sums right today, and I'll help you."

"You are a nice boy today, and you are tidy."

"Be kind to other people and help your mother and grand-mother."

"Don't listen to the devil, be kind to creatures."

"When you go to a party, and your little brother don't, give him a piece of the birthday cake."

"Please help the sick people. Help me to grow more like you."

4. Children making their own prayer book.

A headmistress sent in a beautifully produced book of prayers which her children had themselves written and illustrated. The children made, wrote and illustrated these prayers at home, and then brought them to school, where each child was given the opportunity to stand on a chair and offer his or her own prayer, phrase by phrase.

The prayers, written on small neat pieces of paper, some of them coloured, were artistically fitted into an album with a delicate blue cover, finished with a black bow and ornamented on the front and back with two different and most attractive nativity scenes. Turning the pages, one was struck with the tasteful colouring of the children's work and the harmonious way in which all the contributions blended together. The whole thing was an evident labour of love, and obviously completely real to the children.

Here are a few examples of the prayers:

Dear Father God, I thank Thee for all the things we eat. (With picture of child at table.)
Thank God for the rain and snow and autumn and winter. Also the sun, which helps the flowers to grow.
Dear Father God, thank You for all the lovely coloured fish. (Picture of fish in vivid colours.)
Thank You, God, for everything. I do love You so. Amen.

Dear Father God, I thank You for my home and my mother and father and my brothers. (Picture of house, with family in a line outside it.)

Thank You, God, for our mummies and daddies. Amen.

Dear Father God, I thank you for the kittens and the dogs. (Picture.)

Dear Father God, I love all the things under the water, they are so beautiful; and God made them. Amen. (Colourful picture of starfish and other sea creatures.)

Dear Father God, I thank you for my dear baby. He is so sweet. Amen. (Picture of small girl with baby brother.)

(B) TEACHERS' EXPERIENCES

FROM THE NORTH

My own preparation must be as complete as possible, that is:
a weekly programme of hymns has been chosen, and prayers composed or adapted from various sources—
the music is ready on the piano—

I myself am in the hall as soon as the bell goes in the playground.

Arrangement. The children come in and sit down on the floor, and talk quietly till all have undressed and are in the hall. Soft music calls them, and when the music ends, very softly, I give a sign, and they stand. Next come *greetings*, followed by a *general hymn*, e.g. "Thank You, God of Heaven, for a day begun", or a "story" hymn, such as "Shadows in the Temple place", or "There was a gentle shepherd boy". Next a *prayer* for the season, special occasion, for sick children, children without homes and parents, people who work for us, and so on. This is followed by the *Lord's Prayer* (sung) and the *Blessing.* Then a *second hymn*, a "nature" hymn—"Daisies are our silver"; "Say, little squirrel, are you ready for the winter?"; "See how the snowflakes are falling".

The extended Assembly. On Tuesday and Friday I retain the children in the hall, as the staff have clerical work to do. On Tuesday the larger children sit in a ring on chairs, enclosing the whole company, and we have a story in a sequence—Joseph stories, stories of Jesus, His healings, etc.: a picture to illustrate, or a flannelgraph, unite the children and heighten the listening. On Friday we practise our hymns—we know a great number— with a dozen children as a choir to help. Sometimes we act out little situations involving a moral principle, such as: "What do we do when someone wants us to buy sweets on the way to school?"; "What do you do when you find a penny?"; "What do you do in a bus when you have a seat and a lady with a baby is standing?"; "When you have a good game and someone wants to join in?" The clapping and lit-up faces when the right solution is acted are quite wonderful! Chuckles and "Oo-oo's" come when the children act the "wrong" solution to the question.

My own attitude depends on my entering absolutely into each part, directing my own worship to God Himself, and directing the Blessing at the end to any particular one of the children or staff whose special need is known to me.

Altogether, assembly times and the extended assembly are a very happy affair, an informal time when we enjoy ourselves together, hear each other's news, and feel grateful to be alive in God's world.

FROM THE SOUTH

All the children except the Nursery take part in "Morning Talk", as we call our Assembly; and the members of the Nursery are quite free to do so if they want to. We find they gradually drift in of their own accord at about four years old, but some prefer to go straight to the Nursery and settle down to work.

We always start with a hymn, which the children take it in turn to choose, the "chooser" being responsible for giving out and collecting the hymn books. We use Blackie's *Children's Book of Hymns*. It has all the better-known hymns, and it has very nice pictures, so even the smallest can have a hymn book and find the right picture and not feel left out.

The hymn is followed immediately by a short time of silence, preceded by the words, "Please, God, help us to be still, and to know that You are with us, now and all through the day." Every now and again during the term we have a little talk about this silence, in which I try to help them to understand, as simply as possible, that God is with us and can talk to us through our thoughts, and help us in everything we do through the day. Often the children come to school with no conception of God, and we get the question, "How can God be here?" "We can't see Him." They seem to understand best by first of all realising that they have two parts themselves —their bodies which we can see, and what we call their "thinky part", which we cannot see. After amplifying this idea sufficiently to make sure it is quite understood, they seem able to grasp the idea that God has no body, only the "thinky part", and that He must use our bodies to do His work. I have found that one can help them gradually from this point to know God for themselves, and to begin to receive His guidance.

Sometimes, perhaps when somebody is away ill, a child will spontaneously suggest some prayer, which we all say before we join in the little prayer, given above, with which we start our silence.

On Monday mornings we always have a "news morning". After silence, we have another little time of quiet, this time in order to think about something interesting to tell the School. After that we have "hands up", and take it in turn to tell our little bits, everybody who has anything to say having a chance to take part. When we first started this there was chaos, as everybody wanted to talk at once, and was not the least bit interested in what anyone else had to say; but after we introduced the quiet time to start with, to get our thinking done, they have gradually improved in this respect, and now wait patiently for their turn and really listen to other people's news. I think this time is very valuable, as they get used to speaking freely in front of the whole school, and very soon even the shy ones can't resist telling us some little thing, and gradually become more free and confident.

Friday is "singing morning", when we finish Morning Talk by a sing-song. This varies with the time of year—before Christmas it is carols; in the spring, summer and autumn, *Songs of the Flower Fairies*, for the respective seasons, are first favourites; and we have nursery rhymes, Christopher Robin songs, etc. Always the favourite is *Wise old Horsey* in *The Golden Book of Carols* (Blandford).

On the other three mornings of the week, the opening silence is followed by a story. I use a wide variety of stories for this purpose, many of them, but by no means all, being Bible stories. Perhaps the Blandford Bible story books are the most useful of all. We have also a number of the *Bible Books for Small People*, published by the Student Christian Movement

Press. All books with pictures, such as these, are read "upside down", so that they can see the pictures all the time, and they very soon get to know the stories, and to say them with me as each picture comes along.

I find that some Bible stories are very nicely told in *Bible Stories Retold* and *New Testament Stories Retold* by Margaret McCrea, published by Evans Brothers. We also use *A First Book of Bible Stories* by Mary F. Rolt, published by Black. We also like the Bible stories which appear from time to time in *Child Education*.

Apart from Bible stories, the favourite book is *Happy Families*, a book of simple line drawings describing the activities of Mr. Gimme and Mr. Give. A cheer always goes up when that is produced. The children know it from cover to cover, and it is often quoted during the ups and downs of school life. I fear the tendency is usually to apply it to others, and accuse somebody else of being activated by Mr. Gimme; but with much patient help they are beginning to see that we find the solution to difficulties much more quickly and easily when we say "Sorry" ourselves. Another book they enjoy is Harold Burdekin's *A Child's Grace*, where they say the verses as each lovely photograph appears. We have occasionally read three books by Margaret Tempest in this way—*The Lord's Prayer for Children*, *A Thanksgiving for Children* and *The Christchild*, and the older children like these very much for a change.

Sometimes we have a "funny" story, such as "The Pig Brother". Elizabeth Clark has some very nice ones, which make the children laugh, but teach them something at the same time. We have five of her books, *Stories to Tell*, etc. There is a wide variety of tales in these books, legends, true stories, stories of saints, etc., which I find useful for Morning Talk; but these appeal mainly to the older children.

Sometimes, too, we have a "long story", a chapter a day. The most popular book for this purpose is Enid Blyton's *Land of Far Beyond*. They also enjoy *The Fighting Redbreast*. During the last few weeks before Christmas we always have Enid Blyton's *Christmas Book*, which, as well as the Christmas story, tells a lot about the origin of various Christmas customs.

FROM NORTH WALES

What I really find difficult is to be very simple, yet have an atmosphere of reverence, with such a crowd of children. Bible readings really mean next to nothing to the average Infant, and yet I feel the children need to hear the words of the Bible; so after much thought, the following form of Assembly came to me, and when I have taken Assembly in this way, the children seem interested, alive. One of my staff said one day, "I love prayers, Miss X; and I am often deeply moved by the sincerity and devotion of the children."

First of all I chose several subjects, such as:

Jesus our Friend.	Jesus the good Shepherd.
Following Jesus.	Jesus healing the sick and maimed.
God is love.	Jesus the Friend of all children.
Jesus the Teacher.	God the Creator, etc.

One of these themes I used for several mornings. I tried finding large pictures which illustrated the point. This, I found, helped the children to focus their attention and connect the hymns, the prayers and the reading; though I did not always find it necessary to have a picture.

Next I chose two or more hymns that fitted the idea for the week, and a short Bible reading and prayers, all carrying out the same idea. Here is an example:

Theme. Jesus our Friend.

(1) *Hymn*   Jesus, Friend of little children.
(2) *Bible reading*   Mark 10, 13–16 (Christ blessing the children).
(3) *Prayer* of thanksgiving for Jesus' friendship, or asking for His friendship, and dedicating ourselves to His work.

(4) Sometimes the *Lord's Prayer*, sung.

(5) Another *hymn*.

When the children know the Bible reading, as they often do, they recite the verses with me; or I have a group of them to come out to recite them. They know the verses about the good Shepherd, "The Lord is my Shepherd", and many others.

Sometimes we think, in prayers, of the people who work for us, thank God for the good things they bring us, and ask that those who work in dangerous places may be in God's safe keeping, such as:

> the miners who dig the coal underground—
> the farmers who grow our food in all weathers—
> the fishermen in stormy seas, etc.

Harvest Thanksgiving always means a lot to little children. When the table is laden with all their gifts of fruit, flowers and vegetables they seem to understand so readily God's great care and provision, and are anxious to share what they have with the less fortunate children in an orphanage.

The playing of quiet music as the children come into the hall always helps to create a reverent atmosphere.

FROM LONDON, S.E.

I teach in a London Infants' School. Four days a week I have the two youngest classes (aged 5 years—boys and girls) for Assembly and a Scripture story. The children, about sixty of them, sit in a double semi-circle around the piano. To some extent we follow the pattern of the School Assembly, so that the children get used to the procedure there.

They take their seats and chat. Usually they have news to tell one another, and to tell me, before we can start. Often we discuss clean hands, clean nails, clean shoes and the importance of having a handkerchief. Then we talk about the correct way to sit. Finally we say a formal good morning to each other.

The hymn is then announced, and we stand and sing. This is

usually followed by a prayer and another hymn, and then the story.

One day, I felt that although I said an impromptu prayer, followed by one which we all sing, the children didn't really have a big enough part in the Assembly. So I asked them for ideas on what we should pray for. They came thick and fast: "That God will keep us good"—"keep us smiling"—"help us with our work"; "pray for those who are away ill"; "thank You for a new day"; " make Bobby good" (a troublesome boy), etc. I used these ideas in the prayers.

The next day came the thought to let one of the children do the actual praying. I suggested that one of them might like to say a prayer for us all, and then I would go on with the prayer after him or her. Many hands went up to suggest what to pray for, and to volunteer to say the prayer for us. Kenneth was chosen; and this was his prayer: "Thank You, God, for another new day, and for taking care of us in the night. Help us to be good and do our work." Then I continued straight on.

The next day Maureen prayed for us, though her voice was rather small for us all to hear. She asked God to keep us smiling, and to help us with our work.

Little children are very sincere and reverent when they are actually taking part in the Assembly. It is only when we make it a dead, mechanical routine that it becomes meaningless to them. It can be, and is meant to be, a time of worship and inspiration for teachers and children. The children realise that the teachers are not the final authority, but that they too obey a loving authority. It is at this time, too, that children gain ideas to live by. They are very sensitive to the reality of the teacher's spiritual life. Kindness, unselfishness, honesty, cleanness, all have an important place in the child's religion, and ideas gained in Assembly and the Scripture time are carried through the day, and from day to day.

One day, when reading the story of Moses, we came to the idea that God spoke to Moses. We discussed how He spoke to him, and decided that He put a thought into Moses' mind. We thought that God might have something to say to us too, perhaps about the day. So we had a few moments of quiet, about two minutes, and then talked about what we had been thinking. Some had thought about the story. One boy said he was asking God to make Bobby good! Then one boy volunteered that "he got smacks at home" because he was naughty. That afternoon we asked him if he had had any smacks at dinner time, and very triumphantly he shook his head.

Another small girl said, "My mummy doesn't want me." Her mother is a chronic invalid, unable to walk and often in hospital. I had been praying for Gillian, and trying to see why she was often "catty" with the other children. Only then did I realise how much love she needed, and how much she was missing at home.

The thought which had come to me during the moment of silence was, "Be quiet", and I told the children so. Then, later in the morning, when the children had been rather noisy and I was tempted to be noisy too, in order to get them quiet and listening to me, I reminded them of the thought I had had, and as a result, we had a quiet lesson together.

During the war I had a class of four, five, and six year-olds. Some were village children, others evacuated from London. We pinned a map on the wall, and each had a little flag with our name on it stuck into the place where father or uncle were, in France, Germany or elsewhere. We tried to behave and do our work, feeling we were part of the grown-up world, helping father or uncle, and backing them up by standing our best, or doing what was right, or trying our hardest when there was something difficult to be done.

Here is another five year-old's prayer:

Thank you, God, for the bulbs. Please make us good and happy, and help us with our sums, and help us to be quiet. Thank you for the rain that makes the flowers grow. For Jesus' sake. Amen.

SUGGESTIONS AND EXPERIENCES

FROM NORTH LONDON

I have charge of the Nursery Class—the under fives—in a Junior and Infant School. We do not have any special times of prayer, but they arise out of the various opportunities which occur during the day.

"Thank You" times come very often. The nature table, with its ever-changing bowls of flowers, bulbs, seeds, etc., attracts the children's attention, and it is natural to thank God for their shapes, colours and scents, and for the warm sunshine, the cool wind or the soft snow, according to the weather.

We know Jesus as our Friend and Helper, and say "Thank You" to Him for all sorts of things—mummies and daddies, brothers and sisters, friends, birds and flowers, clothes and toys, happy days, games and fun.

Sometimes we need to have "Sorry" times, when we say "Sorry" to Jesus for things we have done that have made Him sad. The children understand that when we say we are sorry, it makes Him happy again, and then we are happy too. Michael said today, "God doesn't like you any more when you kick", and we had a talk about this, to realise that God loves us all the time, whatever we do—it's the kicking and hurting each other that He doesn't like.

We have "Please" times too, when we ask Jesus to take care of people we love and of children who are ill and have to go to hospital. And we also have times when we not only talk to Jesus; we listen to Him too.

So much depends on the atmosphere the teacher creates. I find that for me the important thing is to have the right relationship with God and with other people, working in harmony with them, and taking full responsibility myself when things go wrong, instead of blaming others. Then there is peace in my own heart, which gives the children security and happiness.

Ours is quite a small school; but we felt we wanted to have a harvest service. I talked to the children about it, and suggested that they might like to bring what they could for decoration. They responded most eagerly, bringing lovely flowers and fruit, with which we decorated the classroom.

We began the service by singing "We plough the fields and scatter . . ."

Then I read God's promise to mankind in *Genesis* 8, 22: "While the earth remaineth, seedtime and harvest, and cold and heat, and summer and winter, and day and night shall not cease."

After this we sang, "Fair waved the golden corn".

I gave a short talk on harvest, something like this: "All the world rejoices over the harvest, and has done so for hundreds of years. All the crops are now safely gathered in. (Here I listed them, the children supplementing with others, such as nuts for the squirrels' stores.)

"The harvest this year is good, because we have had good weather, the right amount of sun and rain, no late frosts to spoil the fruit, or rain and wind to beat down the standing corn. Sometimes, in other years, we have bad harvests, because of rain and frost. But we always find that when there is a bad harvest in one place, there is a good one in another, so that there is enough for all, if people will share." (I elaborated this point a little, to bring out the truth, which is familiar to the children, that there is enough in the world for everyone's need, but not enough for everyone's greed; and that if everyone cared enough, and everyone shared enough, everyone would have enough.)

"The farmers rejoice most over the harvest, because of all the hard work they have put into it." (Again I made a list, with the children's help.) "But all this work would be no good without God, who gives the harvest.

> We plough the fields, and scatter
> The good seed on the land,
> But it is fed and watered
> By God's almighty hand.

"And not only have we this year's harvest, but we have enough over to sow for next year, so that next year's harvest is safe too. And the seed we sow will spring up and bear fruit, some thirty, some sixty and some a hundred fold." (I elaborated and explained this last point.)

The children were most interested, and took a lively part all through.

After the talk, we sang "All things bright and beautiful."

Then the children prayed themselves, as is their custom, simply thanking God for the harvest, and mentioning some of the things of which we had spoken.

After the service there was much discussion as to what was to happen to the fruit and flowers. Several children thought they should be sent to the local maternity hospital, where they were born; others favoured a children's home at Bexhill, seen on their holidays. One small boy suggested that the fruit might be sent to his cousin's school, "because they would like the nice rosy apples so much." Finally one little girl said, "My granny hasn't been very well—she would love to have a parcel." This met with unanimous approval; a nice box was carefully packed, some of the flowers being included, and sent off to the ailing grandmother, with a letter written by the whole school. Needless to say, she was delighted to receive it and wrote back.

Section 9

Calendar of Prayers and Readings

FOR ASSEMBLIES THROUGHOUT THE YEAR

Bibliography

Sing and Pray: Services for the Infant Assembly. Madge Swann. *Blandford.*

The Little Bible. Selections for school and home. *Oxford University Press.*

The Children's Bible. *Cambridge University Press.*

My Bible Book. Joyce L. Brinsley. *Harrap.*

New Testament Stories Retold. Margaret McCrae. *Evans Bros.*

Happy Families. Bradburne and Voller. *Blandford Press.*

A Child's Grace. Harold Burdekin and Ernest Claxton. *J. M. Dent.*

The Christmas Book. Enid Blyton. *Macmillan.*

VERY FIRST BIBLE STORIES. *Blandford Press.*

Baby Jesus—the nativity story.

Zacchaeus—the little man who wanted to see Jesus.

The Little Black Lamb—the story of the lost sheep.

The Little Grey Donkey—the story of Palm Sunday.

The Picnic Boy—the feeding of the five thousand.

The Blind Man who saw Jesus.

The Runaway Son—the story of the prodigal son.

Noah and his Ark.

Moses the River Baby.

Daniel and the Lions.

My Very First Prayer Time Book.

The Three Wise Men.

The Two Little Houses—built on rock and sand.

Jesus and the Little Girl.

The Little Wave.

Joseph the Dreamer.

Jesus and the Four Kind Friends.

The Story of Samuel.

Ten Little Silver Coins—the lost coin.

Jesus at the Wedding Party—marriage at Cana.

The Sower and the Seed.

Jesus and the Poor Widow—widow's mite.

These have been made into film strips by Educational Productions, Ltd.)

Index

POETRY INDEX

INDEX

STORY INDEX

Bible Stories

Other Stories